Merry Christmas

(17th *nei*

your

M

C000260075

meam

X*mas* 2023

The Receipt Book
of
Lady Ann Blencowe

Seventeenth Century Cookery
and Home Medicine
by
Christina Stapley

Cookery Editor

Jackie Wilson

with a

Foreword and

Biographical Note by

Peter Blencowe

Edited

by

Jack Blencowe

Other Heartsease Books
by
Christina Stapley:

Herbcraft Naturally 1994

The Lemonade Tree 1997

Herb Sufficient 1998

Herbwise Naturally 2000

With the exception of those specifically
given as modern recipes, the medicinal
remedies in this book are not suitable for
use today. The author cannot take
responsibility for readers trying them.

© Copyright Christina Stapley 2004.

All rights reserved. No part of this publication
may be reproduced, stored in a retrieval
system, or transmitted in any form or by any
means, electronic, mechanical, photocopying
or recording or otherwise without the written
permission of the author.

ISBN: 0-9522336-5-7

Published by HEARTSEASE BOOKS
5, Cromwell Road, Basingstoke.
Hants. RG21 5NR
Tel. 01256 357547

Printed in Great Britain by
Antony Rowe Ltd, Chippenham, Wiltshire.

Contents

(v)

CB&ECO

(vii)

(viii)

CB80

Recipes for Today

Cakes and Biscuits

Desserts

CR8O

List of Colour Plates

Foreword

Enter any large book shop today and there will be a section devoted to 'Cookery'. This will consist of recipe books by Delia Smith, Jamie Oliver and other famous names. Likewise visit a Garden Centre and there will be an area for 'Herbs and Culinary Plants'. Turn on the television in the early evening and if there is not a quiz programme being shown, the odds are that a cookery demonstration will be on the screen. This indicates that the interest that Lady Ann Blencowe shows in her recipes is as much alive today as it was in the late 17th Century.

However there is a difference in our eating habits. In my young days, over sixty years ago, the 'Lady of the House' was usually in the kitchen preparing the meals, which took place at set times, even, sometimes, heralded by a gong to summon the family. If she didn't cook herself, she, at least, employed a trained cook to do the work and meals were something of an event or celebration. Today many children are allowed to open a packet of crisps, with a fizzy drink and a biscuit just when they are hungry. Sit-down meals, if taken at all, tend to consist of what is loosely known as 'Fast Food', with all the dangers this can cause to the health of a child. This was not a problem in Lady Ann's time, but it is sad to see it happening today. Hopefully though, we may be realising again the importance of a healthy diet, and the interest in recipes, old and new, may be one of the more encouraging signs.

But what of the 'Star' of the book: my 'six-times-great-grandmother,' Ann Blencowe. Her portrait, illustrated in this book, was painted by an artist of the school of Michael Dahl, in the mid sixteen-seventies. We can presume this date is about correct as there is an orange tree in the background of the portrait and Ann herself is holding a sprig of orange blossom in her hand. Orange blossom, at that time, was a symbol of betrothal and therefore it must have been painted just prior to her wedding to John Blencowe of Marston St Lawrence in 1675*.

Ann was the daughter of a distinguished scholar, Dr John Wallis (1616-1703), Savillian Professor of Geometry in the University of Oxford, Fellow of New College, Oxford and a founding Fellow of the Royal Society — the foremost scientific society of the age. A contemporary and collaborator of Robert Boyle and Christopher Wren, some would consider him to be the greatest English Mathematician before Isaac Newton. He was also an exceptional linguist and, developing the skill of deciphering codes, became cryptographer to the Crown. Ann was born in 1656, and clearly inherited some of her father's enthusiasm to unravel some of the mysteries of the natural world.

Her husband John was born in November 1642, a month after the first great battle of the Civil War, fought at Edgehill. He entered Oriel College, Oxford in 1661, matriculating in 1661 at the age of eighteen. He

*The family traces its descent from 14th Century Adam de Blencow of the village of that name near Penrith. For a broad account of the family's history see:

Blencowe, J.W. (ed) 2001 *The Blencowe Families of Cumbria and Northamptonshire and their Descendants* publ The Blencowe Families Association <www.blencowefamilies.com>

Marston Hall was badly damaged by fire in 1920 but the restored building is probably much as Ann Blencowe knew it. (*Photo: Maurine Work, 1998*)

became a student at the Inner Temple in 1663 and was called to the Bar in 1670. He inherited the manor of Marston St Lawrence from his father Thomas who died in 1674, the year before his marriage. John was made a Sergeant of Law in 1689 and served as Member of Parliament for Brackley in Northamptonshire from 1690 to 1695. He became a Baron of the Exchequer in 1696. In part, John's marriage assisted him in his advancement for when the Deanery of Hereford was offered to his father-in-law, Dr Wallis declined it but said:

"I have a son-in-law, Mr Sergeant Blencowe, of the Inner Temple, a Member of Parliament, an able Lawyer, and not inferior to many on the Bench, of a good life and great integrity, cordial to the Government and serviceable to it".

(xv)

With this recommendation John Blencowe was raised to the Bench as a Judge of Common Pleas on 17 September 1697 and knighted three months later. A portrait of Sir John in his Judge's robes, painted by the Dutchman, John Closterman, is still in the possession of the family.

Both Ann's husband, Sir John, and her father, Dr John Wallis lived to a ripe old age, the former 84 years and the latter 87 years. Could it be as a result of sampling the healthful recipes and 'physical cures' described in Ann's Recipe Book written in 1694?

Today we would describe her book as a 'recipe book' but Ann herself called it 'The Receipt Book of Ann Blencowe', and refers to her recommendations as 'receipts'. The word 'receipt' is now largely used to verify a financial transaction, but in the 17th Century, and until quite recently, it was used to describe culinary proposals. Language, as we well know, is never static!

In 1925 a limited edition of 650 copies was printed by the Adelphi Press with an introduction written by George Saintsbury that I would recommend to those who would like to make a deeper study. 'Lady Ann's Receipts' first published in 1694, through to Delia Smith's best selling ones of recent times, have always been a source of practical interest and charm to readers with cooking skills and some with none. Particularly, when, as in Ann's case, they combine 'physical cures' with culinary recipes, which was customary till recent times.

Finally, all readers of this book, and members of the Blencowe Family in particular, are very fortunate in this interpretation by Christina Stapley. 'Tina' has spent more than thirty years growing and studying the history of herbs and gives talks and workshops all over the country on herb cultivation and historical herb uses, including in cookery. She has written three books on growing and using herbs and has just been awarded a B.Sc. (Hons.) Degree in Phytotherapy (Herbal Medicine). As can be seen from this book, she has a special place for Lady Ann's Receipt Book, and it will surely become treasured possession for all Blencowes, and, indeed, for all those interested in cookery and housekeeping in former days.

Peter Blencowe
Walderton,
West Sussex
July 2004

About this Book

My interest in Lady Ann's book began as I searched for period recipes to use at an historical herb workshop. I had been making and sharing some of her recipes for two years when a visitor to my garden offered to send me instructions for whitening cloth written by her six-times-great-grandmother.

When it arrived I was amazed to see it was also by Ann Blencowe. I rang Sue immediately in great excitement and we marvelled at the co-incidence. Introduced to her brother Peter Blencowe, I was delighted to accept their request to interpret Lady Ann's book for modern readers and cooks.

As 'Lady of the Manor' Ann was responsible for planning and supervising preparation of delicious, elegant dishes for entertaining guests. Readers who make her recipes will soon find evidence of her success. She records the names of friends who have contributed recipes and we may imagine these enthusiastic exchanges. For all those recipes I have tested and consider readers may enjoy making and tasting, there is a separate list 'Recipes for Today' on pp *x-xii*. They are grouped under general titles; Cakes, Desserts, etc., to help choosing the best for each occasion. Many are undoubtedly 'special occasion' recipes rich with cream, sugar and eggs, well suited to an earlier lifestyle involving more exercise and more calories burned just keeping warm. The Preserves are excellent and well worth the time taken to make them. Below each modern recipe I have written explanatory notes and comments on flavours.

I wish you joy in exploring Lady Ann's world!

1

To make a sack possett att a wedding

Take a quart of milk, or cream; if milk, take fifteen eggs, if cream, ten eggs: beat them well with the whites. Then putt to them three-quarters of a pint of sack*, and let them stand together till it be almost ready to boyl: then take the milk off ye** fire & pour it as high as you can to ye sack & eggs, & let it stand by ye for half an hour.

Ingredients:

4 eggs
3 fl oz (90 ml) sherry
8 fl oz (240 ml) of milk

Beat the eggs well and add the sherry. Bring the milk almost to the boil over a moderate heat and add it from a good height into the eggs and sherry. Let the mix stand for half an hour, by which time it will have set like a custard. This can be spooned off, or the alcoholic liquor beneath can be drunk through a straw before enjoying the rich topping of curd.

Possets were very popular in Lady Ann's day and for some time after. They were wonderfully nourishing, warming and medicinal strengtheners, particularly for someone unable to digest a full meal. They were also enjoyable. Pouring the milk from on high, as this recipe instructs, brings air into the mixture, making lots

---

*White wine, in those days usually from Spain or the Canaries.

**The 'y' in 'ye' is an Anglo-Saxon abbreviation of 'th' thus would have been pronounced 'the'. Similarly 'ym' would be 'them'. In the same sentence she uses 'ye for 'you'.

of foam. This is a warming winter delight. It may be compared with the also delicious, frothing and alcoholic lemon syllabub on page 70. Sherry may suitably replace sack used in the original; possets were also made with white wine or ale.

∞

A great cake

Take 5 or 6 pounds of currants, pick't, wash'd, & dried, & plump'd if you please, & set them before the fire that they may be warme. Take 5 pound of flower, putt it into a pan. Take sixteen eggs, putt away half ye whites, & beat them very well & strain them & a pint of ale yeeste, stirring together a pint of cream & a pound and half of butter, & putt them together that ye cream may warm ye yeeste & eggs; & with a warm liquor wett ye flower, & when it is mix'd cover it with a warm cloth, & sett it before ye fire, in a pan that you wett it in; & so let it stand, stirring it sometimes that it may be equally warm till ye oven be hott.

Take half an ounce of mace & two good nutmegs, & cinamon or what spice you like best, & half a pound of sugar; & mix it all together, when ye oven is hott, with ye currants as they are warmed, putting it to ye dough, & when it is well mix'd have a large stronge paper, & butter it, & lett it be doubled with a paper hoope. Itt may be bak'd in an hour.

4

Ingredients:

6 oz (170 g) butter
3½ fl oz (105 ml) double cream
2 eggs
2 egg yolks
1½ oz (40 g) golden caster sugar
1 oz (25 g) fresh bakers' yeast or the equivalent dried
12 oz (340 g) good quality, plump currants (mixed fruit can be used if preferred)
1 lb (450 g) plain flour (81% wholemeal)
5 fl oz (150 ml) ale
½ teaspoon grated nutmeg
1 teaspoon cinnamon

Melt the butter and leave to cool. Pour the cream into a large, warmed jug, beat in the 2 eggs, 2 yolks and 2 teaspoons of sugar and pour the melted butter in slowly while stirring rapidly. Lastly, add the crumbled baker's yeast. Set the jug in a warm place for the yeast to start to work.

Weigh the currants and remove any stalks as you spoon them into the mixing bowl. Add the sieved flour and mix. Put these to warm with a cloth over the bowl. When the yeast is frothing in the jug, stir into the flour and currants. Add the warm ale. Leave in a warm place to rise for 45-60 minutes. It should now be doubled in size.

Stir the spices into the remaining sugar and add to the bowl, mixing well. Spoon the fairly thick, elastic mixture into two 16 cm round tins, or one large tin. Leave again in a warm place for a further half an hour to rise.

Bake at 160°C (fan-assisted oven). A 16 cm cake will

take approximately 50-60 minutes to cook. Add approx. 15-20 minutes if cooking in single tin.

The main flavouring for this cake comes from the spices and the ale. The ale makes all the difference between a rather ordinary cake and a very tasty one. The flavour resembles an exceptionally good fruit scone.

CR80

To make Vinegar.

Take two pounds of Malago reasons, & one gallon of spring water, set them (in a pot or vessel cover'd) in ye hot sun for 6 or 8 weeks & it will become Vinegar. You may boyle ye water first & put it hot to ye raisins, & 'twill be vinegar sooner & keep better.

CR80

To make Water Cheese.

Take ye night's & morning's milk, in ye morning, & make a Cheese as usual. But all is in crushing it very well in ye fat, turning it that you may squeese it ye better; but put it not in ye Press. Then lay it in water whole as you take it out of ye fatt.

Ye morning following make another cheese, as before, then drean ye first from ye water, & break them both together in a tub so that no lumps be left, & when 'tis very well broke (for that is a great matter) putt in a little salt (not too much) in ye curd, then putt a wett

cloth in ye fatt, & putt ye curd in it, & with help
crushing it very well; & turn it in ye fat & then putt
in ye press, & when you turn it in dry cloths, salt it
as usual, & take care in turning it, till 'tis dry,
keeping a cloth over it for fear of craking it.

CB80

To make a cheese (Mrs. Bennet)

Take ye night's milke of seven cows, & take ye
creame of it; then take morning milke of 7 cows, &
ye morning milke and ye night's creame together.
Then take a handfull or two of marrigold flowers
well picked & bruised; then boile the marrigolds in a
gallon of watter a whill; then strain the water into ye
said milke & creame & put as much runnet as will
make it com. Covere it close with a blanckett that it
may com hard; & when it is com take two cheese-
cloaths and lay them in two stands, & give your
curd one stirr, & lay in your curd without breaking
of it or sinking of it; then let it stand one houre; then
crush it with bords till ye whay is all out; then lay it
in water halfe an houer; then crush it with bords till
ye whay & water is all out. Then make it up into ye
vatt & put a little salt in ye midle of it; then sett a
fifty pound waight on it for an houer, then shift it
into fresh cloaths every houer for 3 or 4 houers, then
put it into ye press & when you take out of ye press,
salt it, but no tow much; then pinn a cloath about it
to keep it upright till it is stiffe.

To Coller Beef.

Take a piece of Beef of the flanck, and peel off the inner skin, then rub it over with saltpeetr beaten fine, then lay it in strong brine 48 hours; then roll it up with pepper, cloves, and mace, and a little sweett herbs shred very small. When it is fast taped up, put it in a pot, and put in so much smooth strong ale as will cover it. When it is well baked, and so cold as you may well handle it, take off the tape and shape it as you please; then sow it up in a thin cloath very fast and keep it in an upper roome. It will keep in winter a quarter of an year very well.

ᘓᘔ

To Pott Beef.

Take a Buttock of beef, bake it in a pan with nothing to it; when it is baked, take it off from the gravey. When it is cold pare off all the outside, and the fatt, and cutt it with a knife into small bitts, and pound it in a morter. Then take a good handfull of Sage and a little Time shred small, and a little Mace and two Nuttmegs, and a little pepper and salt; mix it and beat it all with the meat, then put in a Laying of Meat, and a Laying of Butter, till your pott is full; squease it close downe, and Bake it again for an hour. When it is cold, power butter upon it and it will keep a good while.

Ingredients:

1 lb (450 g) of beef (tell the butcher it should be buttock)
1 dessertspoon of dripping
1 teaspoon chopped fresh sage
½ level teaspoon chopped fresh thyme (stalks removed)
½ teaspoon grated nutmeg
Pinch mace
8 teaspoons butter

Smear dripping on the beef and wrap it in foil. Bake in a pan in a fan-assisted oven for 45-50 minutes at 170°C.

Remove from the pan and set to cool. When cold, cut off any excess fat and either cut into small pieces and pound as in the original recipe, or use a food blender to reduce the meat to a paste.

Season with sage, thyme, nutmeg and mace. Chop and fold in butter. Beat together in the mixer until it starts to come together. Put into three small ovenproof pots and press down, leaving one-third in (10 mm) at the top to give space for the mix to rise as it cooks.

Set the pots in a baking tin and bake for 35-45 minutes at 150°C. When cold, pour melted butter over the beef to seal. Cover with two layers of greaseproof paper, then foil or a lid. Keep in a cool place.

The layering of butter and meat in the original recipe was only necessary as it involves a very large amount of potted beef being kept in a large pot. This allowed the potted beef to be removed down to the next layer of butter, which then sealed the remainder until the next use.

Ginger Bread.

Take 3 quarters of a pound of sugar, an ounce and half of Ginger, half an ounce of Cinamon in fine pouder. Mingle all these with your flower, and make it up with 3 pound of Treacle, just so stif as will keep it from running about ye board; then put in 3 quarters of a pound of Melted butter, and stirring it well togeather; then strow in some more flower by degrees, enough to make it so stif as will make it up in cakes. The Oven must be no hotter than for manchets*, lett it stand in ye Oven 3 quarters of an hour; wash out the treacle with 2 or 3 spoonsfull of Milk, bake it on butter'd papers; mince in also 2 ounces of Oringe pill, and preserved sittern 2 ounces, and 2 great nuttmegs grated.

Ingredients:

2 oz (55 g) dark muscovado sugar
5 teaspoons powdered ginger
3 teaspoons powdered cinnamon
2 level teaspoons grated nutmeg
8 oz (225 g) black treacle
2 oz (55 g) melted butter
8 oz (225 g) fine SR wholemeal flour
$1/3$ oz (10 g) candied orange peel

Take the sugar and spices and mix with half of the flour. To weigh the treacle leave the scale pan lined with flour, it will then pour out again easily. Pour in

*Small loaves (of the best quality of wheaten bread)

the treacle and mix again. Add the melted butter alternately with the remainder of the flour and candied orange peel. Set to stand in a warm place for 45 minutes. Form into rounds about 2 inches (5 cm) across. Bake on a greased or lined tray for 15-20 minutes at 170°C.

This produces deliciously flavoured but very hard gingerbread. A typical biscuit of the time, possibly produced because they would keep in the less than airtight containers without going soft. They are wonderful, however, when dunked. Some very small biscuit pieces can be made ready to add to the Spanish Custard on page 89.

CX8O

To make Tea Lozenges.

Take of ye leaves of ye Indian Regal, that is of Tea, 1 ounce, watter of Liquid christall, that is fair watter, 10 ounces. Let there be infusion for 6 hours in ye watter strained; adde of suger candy 1 pound. Let it be boyled to a due consistance, then adde of ye forsayd Leaves, in very fine sifted powder, 1 ounce of Pearl perpared, 1 dram of Amber-Greese, half a scruple. Make of this guilt lozenges.

This recipe celebrates a relatively new speciality, Indian tea; thanks to heavy import taxes, though, it was a very expensive speciality. The recipe offers a fascinating glimpse of the fashionable ingredients of the period. The liquid crystal mentioned is simply pure clean water. The inclusion of ambergris should not surprise us for it was frequently put into icings and cakes in upper class kitchens in the 18th century, as well as being used as a perfume. Ambergris may have a more specific link with tea. In The Art of Perfumery (1879), the author recalls hearing that the Chinese added fine scrapings of ambergris to boiling tea. If it dissolved perfectly, the ambergris was judged to be genuine. In Lady Ann's day there was still considerable discussion as to exactly what ambergris was, but it was certainly popular. Pearl was used in some toothpastes soon afterwards, I have not found it in other edible recipes. Present-day cooks will not be able to appreciate this recipe, as we now know that the source of ambergris is an intestinal calculus from the intestines of a whale.

CBEO

Sage Wine.

Take nine Gallons of Spring Watter & let it boyl a quarter of an hour; then take fourty pounds of very good Malaga raisons clean pickt & very fine, shred but not wash'd, & about half a Bushell of red sage shred also, & when the watter is little more than bloud warm, pour it on them & work it with a Porringer of Ale yeest about as warm as you would bear. And let it stand covered warm six or 7 day stirring it once every day & straining it once every day; strain it through a sive or hair bag dry, then put it into a vessel that may be full, & let it work 2 or 3 days. When it has done working stop it up close. You may draw it off in four or five months if it be clear; if you think it fitt to have it stronger, you may put more Raisons in it, but it will be longer before it is ready to drink.

Ingredients:

1 gallon (4.5 litres) water
4 lb 6oz (2 kg) large muscatel raisins
8 oz (225 g) fresh tops of red sage – 6 oz (170 g) after removing the main stems)
1 oz (25 g) fresh baker's yeast
2 oz (55 g) raw cane Demerara sugar

Put the raisins in several batches into a food blender, with a little water with each batch, and blend briefly. Having removed the main stems of the sage, arrange the freshly picked sage leaves in bunches and shred by slicing across the bunches. Put the sage and raisins into the fermenting bucket. Bring the water to the boil and pour all but half a pint (300 ml) over them. Pour the remaining half pint (300 ml) of boiling water into a jug and stir in the sugar until dissolved and leave to cool to blood heat. Stir in the fresh yeast and leave to stand in a warm place for fifteen minutes before adding to the fermenting bucket. NOTE. The contents of the fermenting bucket should also be at blood heat when the yeast/sugar mix from the jug is added.

Cover and leave in a warm place for about nine days. Drain and pour into a clean demijohn until almost full. Fit fermentation lock. Keep at room temperature 3-6 months until fermentation complete. Siphon into bottles and wait for 6 months before tasting. Improves with age.

N.B. Sage Wine should not be drunk in pregnancy

To Make Almond Jumballs.
(Mrs. Bethel)

Take a pound & a half of Almonds. Beat them very fine with Orange flower & Rosewater. Then (if for white) take a pound & 1/2 of Duble refined Sugar, boyl it to a Candy, then take it off ye fire. Putt in your Almonds & break all ye Lumps & stir it over a gentle fire till it be very stiff. And when it is quite cold putt to it a pound & 1/3 more of fine sugar, & ye white of an Egg; mix it well togeather with Your hands, then beat it well in a morter into a past. Then with Your squart make it what forme you please; you may Color some with Chocalett or Cutchaneale. Then wett it with rosewater or juice of Limon; a very gentle oven will Bake them; it is best to sett them on something that they may not touch ye bottome of ye Oven.

CఎEOD

To Pickle Musherrooms

Gather your musherrooms early in the morning, and then throw them into salt and water, and so lett them lye for three hours. Then take a piece of fine flannell and rub the heads of the musherrooms one by one and boyl them off in salt and water; then after you have boyled them put them into fresh salt water, and lett them stand for three days. Then shift them into salt and water again, so serving them so for a month's time, shifting them every three days and when you find them come white, then make your pickle, which is -- one quart of white wine vinegar, one pint of sharp white wine and quart of clear spring water, a small quantity of whole mace, a small quantity of whole ginger and jnon* stuck with a few cloves in it, a little quantity of salt, two or three bay leafs. Then drean your musherrooms from the salt and water, & dry them well with a coarse clothe; then putt them into your pickle and tye them up close.

CӠ♉♈ꙮ

To make peas soope.

Take about two Quarts of peas & boyl them down till they are thick; then put to them a leeke & a litle slice of bacon & a litle bunch of sweet herbs, & let them boyl till they are broke. Then work them with ye back of a ladle thro a coarse hair seive; then take about 3 pints of your peas & mix with about 3 quarts of very strong broth & work them very well together. Then sett them over a Stove & let them boyl very easyly. Then as for your herbs, take to the quantity of a gallon of soope; take a large handfull of spinage & one third of sorrill & one cabbage, Lettice, & a litle Charvell & Creases & a head or two of sallery & Indive, & ye heart of a Savoy, & a litle mint, but mince your mint very small if it be green, but if it be

*onion

15

dry, then drie it before ye fire to powder, & sift it thro
a seive, & mince ye herbs with one leeke very small, &
put them into a brass dish or saspan with half a
pound of butter, & let ym stove till they begin to be
tender. Then put to them a quart of good gravy or
strong broth, but gravy is best, & when you have
mix't it well then putt it into ye pott to ye peas & a
litle beaten cloves & mace. So let it stove about half
an hour, then have a french roll, either dry'd in an
oven or tosted by ye fire, in thin slices, then season
ye soope to your palate & so serve it up. If you please
you may put forcd meat balls into it, or any other
thing, as pallates & sweetbreads or Combs.

The recipe for Pea Soup is not set into modern terms
as it would take too long for most modern cooks to
wish to follow it. The instructions are, however clear,
and for anyone wishing to try it, I would simply point
out that "spinage,... sorrill,... Charvell & Creases,...
sallery and indive" are:- spinach, sorrell, Chervil and
Cresses, celery and endive. The sweet herbs would
have been marjoram, thyme and parsley. The peas
were of course, dried.

CB&O

16

Almond puddings.

Grate a 2 penny loaf. Take ye equal weight of beef suit minc'd & some marrow, half a pound of almonds pounded very fine with rose water, almost a spoonfull of mace cutt very small, 6 eggs & leave of it 2 whites well beat. Mix it with milk or cream boyling hot, sweeten it as you please, & put in a little sack & sweetmeats cut in large pieces. You may sprinkle your puddings with Rose or Oringe water.

Now bread is so small we use a 2 penny loaf & half, to ye same quantity of almonds.

The recipe is considered unsuitable for modern cooks because it contains beef marrow. .

CX8D

To make Apricock Chips.

Take your apricocks pared & ston'd, & cut every one into 8 peices, & take to a pound of apricocks a pound of sugar & half a pint & two spoonfulls of water, beaten very well with the white of an egg. Wett your sugar with some of the water & when it begins to boyl throw in the rest by a spoonfull at a time, not too fast, stirring it not att all. When it is enough take it off the fire & take off the scumm; sift the sugar very fine, then take the apricocks & put them to the sugar. Let them boyl a litle & scum them, then take them up one by one and lay them in a basin & pour the liquor upon them, scalding hot. So lett them stand two days and two nights, then lay them on a haire seive & let them draine twelve hours, then take them off & put them on a pie plate & sett them in an oven just warm, sifting sugar on them.

Ingredients:

For each pound (450 g) of apricots:
1 lb (450 g) golden caster sugar
½ pint (300 ml) plus two dessertspoons of water
1 egg white.

Peel and stone the apricots, cutting each one into eight equal segments, as if it were an orange. Pour the water into a bowl, add the egg white and beat well. Pour into a thick-bottomed pan with a little of the sugar; when it begins to boil, add the rest of the sugar, a little at a time, without stirring. The egg white will gradually gather on the top. When all the sugar is in and dissolved, remove the pan from the heat and skim off the egg white.

Take the apricot segments and add these to the pan. Return the pan to the heat and bring the apricot mix to the boil, allowing it to boil for no more than 1 minute. Remove the pan from the heat and lift the apricot pieces carefully out of the pan using a slotted spoon or two forks. Place the apricot pieces in a wide casserole dish and pour the liquor, still scalding hot, over them. Cover.

Let them stand covered for two days and nights and then remove the apricot pieces and lay either on a fine cake rack or muslin laid over a cake rack. Allow to drain for 12 hours before setting them on a pie plate in the oven on the lowest setting, having sifted sugar over them. Leave in the oven for about 2 hours, turning once, until dry to touch.

These are quite delicious and will keep for months packed away in chocolate boxes. They can be used to decorate desserts or cakes, or eaten as sweets.

CB&ED

To make Quince Chipps.

Scald the quinces, but not too tender, then pare them & slice them thin & throw double refin'd sugar upon them, when they are layd in a pewter dish with sugar upon them one by one. Then sett them over a very gentle fire till they be just warm; let them stand till the sugar is melted, then put them on the fire & put them all together in the middle of the dish till the sugar creams. Then dip them into the sirrup & lay them on the brims of the dish a-drying & as they dry dipp them again into the syrrop till they have taken up all the syrrup, keeping them all the while over a gentle fire.

Put the quinces whole into a pan and cover with water, bring them to the boil and boil for 1 minute only. Set aside. This will make it easier to peel them. Peel, slice thinly and scatter them with golden caster sugar one at a time, so that they do not become discoloured as they are exposed to the air. Lay the quince slices onto a large ovenproof dish, turn them and scatter with sugar again. Set the dish over a pan of boiling water until the sugar has melted. Spoon all the melted sugar and quince slices into the centre of the dish and heat until the sugar forms thick, white foam. Having made sure the quince slices are coated with syrup, set them one at a time at the edge of the dish to dry a little, before dipping them again. When the slices have taken up all the syrup, remove the dish from the heat and set the quince chips in a warm place to dry before packing in boxes.

> *Not many people have the opportunity to eat quinces nowadays. To achieve the true, quite powerful flavour, use quinces* (Cydonia oblonga) *fresh from your garden in autumn rather than the related Japonica* (Chaenomeles japonica) *fruit. Both are edible and are rich in pectin for jams. Quinces are very fragrant as they are ripening.*

> *Quinces were popular at this period but they are hard fruits. This recipe could be used to crystallize slices of other fruits, but for apricots I prefer Lady Ann's recipe for Apricock chips.*

CB80

To Preserve Apricocks Ripe.

Make jelly of pippins with some apricocks sliced in among the apple to make it taste. Then take your best apricocks, stone them & paire them into water; take their weight in sugar & wett it with water as you paire them; then weigh them, and to every pound of apricock a pound of sugar, and wett it with fair water & boyl it almost to a candie. Then put in your apricocks & half a pint of liquor to boyl them pretty fast till ye apricocks be tender, then take them up &

lay them on stone plate to drain, & boyl the jelly a little after you have taken up your apricocks. Then put it into shallow glasses. Let it stand all night in a dry place. The next day, when it is jellyed, putt your apricocks in glasses & lay ye jelly upon them. For ye half pint of liquor you must allow the weight in sugar & boyl it with ye other sugar before you put in the fruit.

This is quite delicious, but very sweet. You will notice I have already omitted the sugar Lady Ann has written as an afterthought – the weight in sugar of the apple liquor. The recipe does not need this in order to set. This preserve is perfect for stuffing the Bombard Apples (see page 90) or adding in small quantity to sweeten any dessert. The apricots are beautifully preserved to use as a rich, colourful decoration to flans or trifles.

Ingredients (makes approx. 2lbs.)

2lb (900 g) cooking apples
1lb (450 g) golden caster sugar

Wash and chop the apples into quarters, or six pieces each, according to size. Put these with the sliced apricots into a large pan with three quarters of a pint (450 ml) of water. Partially cover the pan and set over a moderate heat to boil until the apples are mushy. Remove from the heat and pour into a jelly bag set over a large jug. Leave to drain for a few hours.

When you have half a pint (300 ml) of apple and apricot liquor in the jug, take the remaining pound (450 g) of apricots and put these into a pan. Cover with water and bring to the boil. Boil for about 1 minute, keeping the apricots whole and firm. This will make it easy to remove the skins, rather than laboriously peeling them. Skin, halve and stone them. (*The stones can be saved to use their kernels for making Ratafia Biscuits, see page 41*).

In another pan add one pound of sugar to a little apple and apricot liquor. Heat gently to dissolve the sugar and then boil fast so that it appears as white, creamy foam. Add the stoned apricots and boil until they are tender, but not breaking up. Strain them out with a slotted spoon and set them on a pie-dish or plate. Cover when cold. Add the remainder of the apple and apricot liquor to the sugar syrup and bring to the boil again. Boil for five minutes and scum. Pour a little into your jars or shallow dishes and leave to set for an hour or so, or overnight. Keep the rest in the pan.

When the jelly in the jars is set, add a layer of candied apricot halves on top of the jelly. The remainder of the jelly can be heated and poured over the fruit, being left to set again. Shallow dishes are no longer a usual container for preserves. You may therefore prefer to heat the remainder of the jelly, adding fruit and jelly in several layers, with each layer of fruit being added to jelly that has already set. Finish with jelly and seal as for jam.

CZ8O

To Preserve Morello Cherrys.

Take a little liquor with water and codlins, then stone your cherrys & put them into that liquor & sett them over the fire to scald till so much of ye dark red be taken out as you like. Then pour them into an earthen dish and let them lye in that liquor till you prepare a jelly for them made strong. Of codlins or pippins take such a quantity as will fill your glasses, then take ye weight of them & ye weight of ye jelly in sugar & something more. Put the sugar into the preserving pan & put the apple liquor to it. When it is wetted sett it on the fire & when it boyls scum it; clean & putt in. your cherrys & boyl them fast till they be tender & look clear, & if your jelly look too pale take so much of the liquor the cherrys were boyld in as will give it a colour to your liking. When they are almost boyld enough, putt in two or three spoonfuls of juice of raw currants & let that boyl a little. But if it boyl too long 'twill give it a burntish taste. When you fill ye glasses first fill them but half full & lett them stand a while, for if you fill them up at once 'twill make them rise too fast; proportion ye jelly to your glasses you think your cherrys will fill.

Ingredients:

7 medium sized cooking apples,
1lb (450 g) cherries
2lb 8oz (1.4 kg) of golden or white caster sugar.

Wash the apples and chop them into quarters, removing any stalks, but leaving the core and pips in. Put these into a pan with one and a half pints of water. Boil them in the partly covered pan until they are mushy. Pour apples and liquor into a jelly bag set over a large bowl. Have this where you can leave the bag hanging for a further couple of hours to drip. This can be done overnight.

Pour three quarters of a pint of apple liquor into a pan, cut the cherries in half, removing the stones and put them into the apple liquor as you do so. Put the pan on the stove and bring the cherries to the boil. Pour them into a dish or jar and cover.

Pour 16 fl oz (475 ml) of apple liquor into a large pan and gradually add the sugar, dissolving it over a low heat. Strain the cherries from their juice and add. Boil until they appear like glacé cherries. Set to cool. Prepare your jars and remove the scum from the jelly before spooning it into the jars in stages. If a little of each jar is filled at a time it helps to stop all the cherries rising to the top.

CR8O

To preserve Lemons in Cloves.

You must pare them very close. Part ye cloves, then scrape all ye white off, but have a care not to break ye cloves when you scrape them. Take out all ye seeds, then weigh them & take their weight in sugar. To a pound of sugar half a pint of water. Sett all on a slow fire & keep them covered with syrup & paper, but let them not boyl. So sett them by till ye next day; then heat them again as you did before, & when you think their sowrness is pretty well out, they are enough. Then make a Jelly with pipins & put them in. So let them have one boyl. Then glass them. They must not stand upon the fire above an hour att a time. The cloves of ye Lemon must be taken clean from ye syrup to put to ye jelly.

Ingredients:

To make 1½ lb (680 g), you will need sufficient lemons to weigh at least ½ lb (225g) once pith and peel are removed (two large and one small lemon may be enough)
Golden caster sugar
3 large cooking apples
1 pint (600 ml) water

Remove the peel from the lemons using a potato peeler (the peel can be dried or candied for future use). With a sharp knife, carefully pare away the white pith, without cutting into the fruit. Part the 'cloves' or segments of the lemon with your fingers and peel away any long strings of pith left. Only open the skin to push seeds out; do not peel the segments.

Weigh the segments and set these aside. Take the same weight of sugar and to each pound of sugar add ½ pint (300 ml) of water. Put the lemons, sugar and water into a pan. Dissolve the sugar over a low heat, and then simmer for a further 5 minutes. Pour into a dish, cover and set aside for the next day.

Wash 3 large cooking apples and quarter them into a pan, pour over ½ pint (300 ml) of water. Boil until the apples are mushy. Put the apples and liquor into a jelly bag and hang to drip overnight.

Next morning, set the lemon segments to reheat in their syrup for about 15 minutes; set a timer to remind you and do not allow them to boil. While they are re-heating, measure the apple liquor and add one cup of sugar to each cup of juice. Heat slowly to dissolve the sugar and, once the sugar is dissolved, turn up the heat and fast boil for 5-10 minutes until a little set onto a cold saucer will wrinkle against your finger once it has cooled. At this point, strain the lemon segments from their syrup and add them to the apple jelly. Bring this back to the boil. Set aside to cool a little before spooning into sterilized jars and sealing.

As always with Lady Anne's recipes, the jars of pre-serve look very elegant and inviting. The syrup from the lemon segments can be saved to add flavour to desserts. Note that the cloves here refers to lemon segments. These are delicious served with Mrs. Harvey's Pancakes on page 42.

CX℘

A shakeing pudding.

Take a quart of Cream, boyle it with spice & salt, & when it is cold put in the yolks of 3 egges & a quarter of a pound of allmons & little grated bread & a little flower & sweten it to your taste.

Ingredients:

1 pint (600 ml) double cream
1½ teaspoons cinnamon
2 pinches grated nutmeg
Pinch of salt
2 egg yolks
2 oz (55 g) ground almonds
2 tablespoons finely ground brown breadcrumbs
1 tablespoon cornflour
1 tablespoon golden caster sugar.

Pour the cream into a pan, adding the spices and salt. Bring almost to the boil. Set to cool. When it is cold, add the egg yolks, stirring well in, and then the ground almonds, breadcrumbs, cornflour and sugar. Pour into individual dishes and leave in a warm place to set for six hours. Alternatively, serve into ramekins and place in the oven at 50°C for 30 minutes. They will set more as they cool.

This spiced custard pudding is tasty served with raisins.

CR80

To make Orange Cakes.

Take Oranges of ye deepest Colouring you can gett &
lay them in water a week, shifting them twice a day.
Then take out the inside & strain out ye juce with
your hands. Cut them in halfs, then take the halfs &
boyl them very tender & lay them to drain till they
are cold. Then pair off ye outside pile very thin, then
pick out all ye seeds & strings; cleave & beat ye
oringes very small in a mortar of stone, then take ye
clearest apple johns & pare & quarter them, but not
cover them, putting them into fair water as you pare
them; put them into as much water as will cover
them, then set them on a quick fire & boyl them till
ye water be consum'd & ye apples grown drie. Then
take them off ye fire & putt them into a hair sieve, &
let ye clear run from them & with a spoon rub ye
apples through ye seive. Then take to half a pound of
beaten oringe a pound of beaten apple, & half a pint
of orange & lemon juce. Mix all these together and
put them into a Silver Basin.

*This is a clear recipe should anyone have the time and
inclination to try it.*

CB&O

Marrow Pudding.

Take a quart of cream boyled & cold, and 12 eggs
well beat, leave out 4 whites: slis 4 biskits and 4
Orangs pile & lay them in a dish fit to bak it on & a
few Currants: the marrow out of 2 bones : sweeten it
as you please: half a houer will bake it.

*The marrow here refers to marrow from bones rather
than the vegetable. If anyone has the taste for such a
fatty dish, this is an easy recipe to follow. It is a fore-
runner to a suet pudding.*

CB8O

To Pickle Walnuts.

Take walnuts att their full bigness before ye shells
are hard so that you may easily run a pin through
them, & cut a little hole in ye side & pick ye kernell
out. Then put them into a kettle of water & let them
hang over a gentle fire for 3 quarters of a hour, but
not quite boyle. Then put them into water & salt & let
them lye nine days. Then take some Garlick, Shelot,
mustard seed, Nutmeg, Mace, cloves, peper, Ginger,
beat together in a Morter & with that [?] ye kernels of
ye walnut. Then take some vinegar & boyle it a litle
with hollspice & little garlick & shalot & let it stand
till it is cold, & then put in your wallnutts to keep for
your use.

CB8O

A puding that eattes like Marro.

Take a pound of beaf suet, half a pound of reasons stoned, 3 spoonfuls of shuger, & 3 spoonfuls of flower, 6 egges, & Nutmeg & salt. Beat ye egges flower & suger together, & let ye puding boyl 5 or 6 hours.

A simple recipe.

☙

To make good Ink.

Take 4 ounces of Galls beaten fine, put them into a bottle of strong beer 4 days, shaking the Bottle 2 or 3 times a day, then put in two ounces of Coperus & one ounce of Gum Araback, When it is too thick fill it up with strong or small beer.

It was not unusual to write all kinds of useful recipes in a household book amongst the cookery recipes, just as we would jot something down in a handy notebook today. The ink is not a blue food colouring and definitely not for eating! The galls referred to were oak galls; all were imported until the 19th century when the gall wasp was imported to make them in this country. Coperus is copper sulphate obtainable from dye suppliers as a mordant and the Gum Araback is gum arabic obtainable from shops selling cake icing equipment and accessories. I have made this ink with native galls but it is not outstanding. It would probably be better with the correct galls. Readers who wish to experiment should note that copper sulphate is currently regarded as hazardous to handle.

For a Tansy.

Take a quart of cream, a pint of juse of spineg, & a little Tansy, half a pound of Napleis biskets & 2 over, 16 eggs & half ye whites, suger, & Nutmeg as you please & stir it over ye fire till it is thick. Then turn it into a dep intermes & set it into ye oven & put some into cokle shels to garness ye dish.

Ingredients:

1 oz (25 g) of any plain sweet biscuit
2 dessertspoons golden caster sugar
¼ pint (150 ml) double cream
2 egg yolks
1 egg white
2 fl oz (60 ml) spinach juice (made by squeezing 6 oz (170 g) thawed frozen spinach through a jelly bag).
1-2 teaspoons chopped tansy
Nutmeg to taste

Grind or crush the biscuit to a powder and add with the sugar to the cream. Stir in the beaten egg yolks and white, then the spinach juice. Add tansy and season with grated nutmeg. Put all the ingredients into a pan over a moderate heat. Stir until the mixture thickens. Turn into a deep casserole dish, cover, and put into a fan-assisted oven at at 50°C to bake for three-quarters of an hour.

Caution: pregnant women should not eat tansy. Tansy recipes containing varying amounts of actual tansy had been popular for several hundred years at the time of Lady Ann. Gradually, less and less tansy was included. Here, it has been largely replaced by the spinach juice, giving a lovely, soft colour.

CB80

To Make Bisketts, Mrs. B.'s way.

Take a pound of fine powder shugar, put it into a stone morter & brake into it 5 egges, leaving out 2 whites. Then beat them very well & put in 6 spoonfuls of Rose watter, & beat it very well againe till all ye lumps be broken, & then strike in by degrees a pound of fine flower, wanting 3 spoonfuls, & beat all together for half an houer, or not so much if your Ovon be hott. Let your Ovon be heating all ye while, if not before you go about them. When your ovon is hott, put in 2 spoonfuls of caraway seeds or ye pell of a Lemon greated & put a spoonfull into a plate, being butterred, & scrape over them a littil fine sugar when it gos in. As soone as they are a littill yellow, cut them out. If you lay them when warm it will be ye better.

This recipe is reminiscent of one for Prince Bisket in Sir Hugh Platt's Delights for Ladies *published in 1603. To the modern cook, it may be appreciated as a very light biscuit, towards the flavour of a macaroon, despite the absence of almonds. Very tasty.*

Ingredients:

¼ lb (120 g) golden caster sugar
1 egg + 1 egg yolk
1½ teaspoons rosewater
4 oz (120 g) white self-raising flour less
¾ dessertspoonful ground caraway **or**

32

grated peel of 2 lemons and caraway seeds (optional)

Beat the eggs well with the sugar, then add the rose-water and beat again. Add the sieved flour steadily and beat all together for half an hour, or 3-5 minutes in an electric mixer. Add ½ teaspoon of ground caraway **or** the grated lemon peel. Ladle ½ dessertspoonfuls of the mixture onto a well greased or lined tray, with a little sugar sprinkled on each. If using lemon peel, a few pounded caraway seeds can be sprinkled on top of biscuits. Put into a moderate oven (170°C for fan-assisted) on a low shelf for 10-12 minutes — until golden.

CB&O

To make Buns Marston way.

Take two pounds and a half of flower well dryed, then rub in half a pound of butter; take a pint of good milk warmed, six or seven spoonfulls of Ale yest not bitter, five Eggs yoalks and whites: strain these through a seive, then mix them well into your flower, and let it stand by the fire half an hour to rise. Then mix in half a pound of Sugar, some Currons or Carraway seeds, which you like best, and a nuttmeg grated, then put it in pattipans or tins as you intend to bake it.

Ingredients:

¼ pint (150 ml) milk
1 tablespoon fresh baker's yeast **or** 2 tablespoons dried yeast
4 oz (120 g) golden caster sugar
10 oz (285 g) 81% SR wholemeal (**or** half wholemeal,

half white SR flour)
2 oz (55 g) butter, 2 eggs
1½-2 oz (40-55 g) currants
½ teaspoon grated nutmeg (optional)
½ teaspoon ground caraway (optional)
Makes 30.

Warm the milk, pour into a warmed jug and add the fresh or dried yeast with 2 teaspoons of sugar. Set this in a warm place to work. Meanwhile, rub the butter into the flour. Beat the egg and add to the flour and butter, along with the milk now frothing from the activity of the yeast.

Mix well, the mixture should be fairly moist — with some flours you may need to add a little extra warm milk. Stand the bowl in a warm place for half an hour for the bun mixture to rise. Stir in the warmed sugar, currants and flavourings. Put into bun tins and bake at 160°C for 15-20 minutes.

These were described by one eager taster as resembling a sweet and spicy Yorkshire pudding — and yummy!

In the original recipe you are directed to strain the eggs. This was a common way of preparing them and the eggs would be strained through a natural sponge – Cleaning the sponge afterwards must have been difficult. Today, we can use a whisk or blender.

ⓒ℘Ⓞ

Flumery ditto.

Boil a quart of cream with sugar lemon peele and all sorts of spice. Then have ready one ounce and a half of Icinglass boild in a little spring water, put it to your cream, and give it two or three boils. Then strain it through a lawn sive, put it in a dish & when cold it will be quite stiff. If you have any moulds put it in them & when cold dip them in hot water & turn them out.

Ingredients:

$^1/_3$ of a teacup of water
¼ oz (8 g) of isinglass
8 fl oz (240 ml) single cream
4 good dessertspoons golden caster sugar
Grated peel of 1 lemon
¼ teaspoon ground, fresh or dried rosemary
½ teaspoon cinnamon **or** ground caraway
Serves 2-4

Set the isinglass in a small heatproof bowl, with about one-third of a teacup of water that should just cover it. Put the bowl over a pan of boiling water and stir until the isinglass becomes a softened gel. Bring the cream, sugar and flavourings to the boil in another pan. Pour in the melted isinglass and beat until mixed. Bring the mixture to the boil two or three times, and then strain through clean muslin or a jelly bag – you will need to push it through. Put it into moulds or a single dish. When cold it will be quite stiff and resemble blanc-mange. If you use moulds, make sure these are simple shapes and not too intricate.

This is a favourite dessert and much enjoyed. The fresh ground rosemary gives a delicate green colouring that is very attractive. The isinglass comes from the swim bladders of certain fish and is available by mail order from Baldwins, London.

CB8O

The Short Cakes Made at ye Bathe.

Take a pound of flower & rube into it half a pound of flower butter very fine; then putt in half a pound of flo sugar & wet it with white wine to a paste; then rowl it very thick & cut it round with ye top of ye Drudger, & knotch it round with a squer & bake them upon tin.

Ingredients:

4oz (120 g) butter (preferably layered with fresh red rose petals overnight)
8 oz (225 g) wholemeal self-raising flour
2 oz (55 g) rose sugar or golden caster sugar
1 fl oz (30 ml) white wine, excellent if home-made primrose or rose

Rub the butter into the flour until it resembles fine crumbs. Stir in the sugar and add sufficient wine to make a thick paste-like pastry. Roll it out as a thick round and cut out round biscuit shapes (about 2½ inch or 65 mm diameter). These need to be about ⅜ in (10 mm) thick as the paste will spread as it cooks. Mark each biscuit with notches at intervals around the edge. Bake at 170°C for 15-20 minutes.

Using the flower butter, sugar and wine makes this a really individual recipe. Plain butter and sugar can also be used with a rose wine. The roses used for flavouring should be Rosa gallica officinalis *or a heavily scented old red rose such as* Rosa damascena, **always be careful that no-one has sprayed the roses with chemicals when gathering them for food.** *To make rose sugar, cut off the white heels of the petals and grind one cup of petals to one cup of golden caster sugar. If you are not using immediately, dry the sugar on a tray lined with greaseproof paper in a 'just warm' oven before storing in a screw-top jar. Grind again before using.*

CB8O

Sweet Water.

Take a galon of fair running Water, one handfull of red rose leves, 2 handfull of rosemary leves, & 2 handfull of Bay leves, half a handfull of Lavender flowers, one Ounce of Cypress roots, 2 Orange pills, 1 pint of Alcorne : put all these together in an earthen pot. Let it stand a week & then Distill it in a Cold still.

It would be lovely to be able to make this aromatic water but the modern house does not have a stillroom, much less a still. It would be a beautiful blend with the herbs and orange peel.

CB8O

To Make Clear Cakes.

Draw ye juce of what you would make them of, in a
gallepot* being set in water as you do for jelly. Then
take ye waight of it in suger, dip ye pieces of suger
in water & put them into your preserveing pan, &
when it is melted over a gentall fire & skimmed, boyl
it up hastily as you can till it be allmoste suger
againe. Then put in your juce & let it stand over ye
fire till all ye suger be desolved (but be sure it does
not boyle); then put it into sawsers & when it is throw
cold, put it into a stove, which you must allways
keep in a temperet heat: if ye stove be too hoat you
spoyle them. When they are all dry & crusted over
turn them upon glass plates : when they are crusted
on both sides box them.

Weigh the pure fruit juice you wish to use (choose a
tart flavour such as blackcurrant, raspberry, strawberry, lemon or orange), and pour it into either a bowl
over a pan of boiling water or a double boiler. Add the
same weight of golden caster sugar. Keep the heat
regulated as the sugar melts, so that the juice does not
boil. When the sugar has dissolved, pour the thick
syrup into small dishes and leave until cold. There
should be about ½ in (12.5 mm) of syrup in the bottom
of each dish; if it is too thin it will be too sticky and difficult to manage. Place the dishes in the oven set on 50-
100°C for several hours, leaving the oven door slightly
ajar. Check at intervals and when the jellies are dry and

*A small glazed earthenware pot, perhaps a ramekin?

look crusted, take a knife around the edge of each and turn them onto a saucer; they will keep their shape and have an intense fruit flavour, resembling a modern clear jelly. However these 'clear cakes' are not sweet and all the rich colour, goodness and flavour of the fruit you have used will be captured inside. Return them to the warm oven until the other side is dried. Store in boxes wrapped in greaseproof paper and bring out on special occasions to add colour to an elegant display of desserts.

> The initial boiling and skimming of the sugar was simply to clean it. Modern sugar does not need this and so it is omitted.

> Marmalades and some fruit preserves would have been kept in boxes of thin wood at Lady Ann's time. You may still occasionally find one used for gift presentation of biscuits or other foods in this country or on the Continent. Plastic containers are not the same but can be substituted.

CK80

To Collor a Pigg or a breast of veall.

Boone your Pigg or veall & season it with Cloves, Mase, Nutmeg, peper & salt, Sweet margeram, time, a letel sage, & role it up as you do brane & boyle it in milk & water very tender. Make a pickle one part water & 3 parts vinegar & all sorts of hole spises, a handfull of sallt, & boyl it & stand till cold before you put in your pigg.

The collar refers to tying and rolling the meat. It was then pickled, a process no longer necessary as we enjoy the benefits of refrigeration. This is an unlikely recipe for a modern kitchen.

Cʒᴇᴏ

A Jelle Tort farmebrough* way.

Make ye cruse cold, take 3 quarters of a pound of Butter to a pound of flower, putt itt into a pattipan that is not too deep. Then take pippins, pair them & slice them very thin into ye pye, and strew some Leamon pill cutt very small & some fine sugar between every roe or two of ye Apple. Then bake itt. When itt is enough take itt out of ye oven & cutt off ye lid. Have in a readiness some John apple Jelley, which pour on ye top & putt your pye into ye oven again a little while.

This appears to be an early form of a flan using a top pastry crust to keep the apple from drying as it cooks. The apple jelly is only lightly cooked and still gives an elegant appearance, something Lady Ann always seeks.

Cʒᴇᴏ

*Farnborough is about 8 miles NW of Marston Hall. Lady Ann's eldest son John married Jane Holbech of Farnborough and lived there. The recipe may have come from his in-laws.

Ratafea Biskett.

Take a pound of double refined sugar, beate & sifted,
5 cournills of Apricocks Blanched & beat very small.
Soake some gum dragon in orange flower water all
night; ye next morning strain out about as much as
a walnutt, ye white of an egg beat to a froth; mix all
these together & drop them on papers, butter, & sift
some sugar over them. Let ye oven be pretty hott.

Ingredients:

5 apricot stones
2 teaspoons gum tragacanth
1 large egg
1 tablespoon orange-flower water
12 oz (340 g) white caster sugar

Take 5 fresh apricots and slice open to reveal the stones
inside. Remove the stones, clean them and open, either
with a nutcracker or by wrapping the nuts in a clean
cloth and banging with a pestle or rolling pin two or
three times. Remove the white almond-like kernels and
place in a small dish. Pour over boiling water to blanch
them and, when cooled a little, remove the skins.
Pound the peeled kernels to a pulp.

It is not necessary to leave the gum tragacanth soaking
overnight.

Beat the white of the egg until frothy. Sprinkle on the
gum tragacanth powder and stir in a little at a time, fol-
lowed by the apricot kernel paste and orange-flower
water. When fully mixed, add the sugar a little at a
time. You may not need quite as much sugar according

41

to the size of your egg. This forms a fairly stiff paste that should just drop off the spoon. Put onto a greased or lined baking tray half a teaspoonful at a time. The paste spreads as it cooks and these are best as small biscuits. Bake at 180°C for about 14 minutes.

These biscuits look elegant and are very suitable for a special-occasion tea. Half the quantity would be sufficient for most people unless they are entertaining; however, the biscuits do keep well in a tin. They are rather like a cross between a meringue and a macaroon as the apricot kernels give a wonderful almond flavour. Since they are almost solidly sugar beware of eating too many! Orange-flower water can be bought from supermarkets and is readily available. Gum tragacanth is stocked by shops selling items for decorating cakes

☙❧

Mrs. Harvey's Pancakes.

Take 3 pints of creame or good milk, putt in half a pound of butter, sett itt over ye fire till ye butter is melted putt in a little mace & cinamon beat very fine, 9 eggs, & when itt is almost cold putt them into ye creame. Stirr in about 3 spoonsfulls of fine flower, fry them in a dry pan as thin as possible; as soon as that side next ye fire is browne, turne itt out upon ye wrong side of a pewter plate, & so throw them one upon another, ye brown side being still uppermost. Till you have fryed itt all you must strew a little sugar between every pan cake.

Melt the butter in the milk with the spices over a moderate heat. Set to cool. Beat the eggs and add with the sieved flour.

Do not try a dry frying pan. Have the pan very hot and greased lightly. Spoon a small amount of mixture in, adding more to it. This makes delicious small pancakes. Serve with the preserved lemons on page 25.

A modern reader may wish to divide the quantities by three. It should be remembered when doing this that Lady Ann's pint consisted of 16 fl oz (475 ml) only, rather than the modern 20 fl oz (600 ml). The amounts will be 16 fl oz (475 ml) milk, 2 2/3 oz (70 g) of butter, 3 eggs, 1 tablespoonful of fine flour and spices to taste.

CB80

To Make a little Pye for an Entermess*.

Take a small Chicken, season it with peper, salt & spice. Then have your paty Ready to put it in with puff paste crust, lay in bits of butter in ye bottom, then put in your Chicken. Have paletts & swetbreads seasoned & a lettell forst meat, strow them in, & 2 or 3 larks with forst meat in their bellys, with ye same seasoning as your Chicken, & so lay bets of fresh butter & then strow palets & sweetbreads again with a litel forst Meat and ye tops of sparograse or scalded spinage. If you pleas you may put a blade of Mace att ye top & some bits of butter. Then close it & bake it. When it comes out of ye Oven have ready a very

*Entremess: served between the courses of a banquet; O.E.D. says 'a spectacular interlude'!

good Gravy fit for ye purpose, with a spounfull of White Wine, Leomon, or pickled barbarys, & some bits of bakon in dice, then cut up yr Pye, & put all in & shak it to close it, & send it to table for a side dish. Your Pallets & swetbreads must be very well boyled before you put them in : ye bacon should be baked in ye pye.

This recipe reminds us that the nursery rhyme about 24 blackbirds baked in a pie was not fanciful: such pies were once baked. In this case, the pie contained larks. Thankfully for these beautiful birds, tastes have changed.

CʒƏɔ

To Fry Oisters.

When they are dried with Cloth, dip them in ye yolkes of egges, cream, & greated bread. Fry them in a good quantity of boyling hot driping & fry them a pall brown : you need not turn them if you have suett enough to cover them.

The 'hot driping' in this recipe refers to dripping — the fat poured off after roasting a joint of meat. A modern cook might well prefer to use olive oil.

CʒƏɔ

To Broyle a Carp.

Lett your Carp be scaled, washed, & scoured cleane
from ye slime & blood. Then scarbanada* it on bothe
sides, wash it over with butter & season ye
scarbanada with time, Nutmeg, & salt. Then put it
on your grid iron & boyle it sloly over charcoals. Keep
it basting. You may broyle some Collops of gammon
with it. Sett uppon ye coals in a stewing dish a
quarter of a pint of Claret, a little Oyster Licker,
Minced Oysters, & hard eggs, with a hanfull of
prans. When your carp are Broyled dish them up &
Garnish them with fryed Collops of gammon & pour
on your licker, being thickened with a ladelfull of
Brawn butter.

Take a scaled, washed fish that has also been gutted
and cleaned inside. 'Scarbanada' is to prepare the fish
for grilling by making a series of cuts through the skin
on both sides of the fish. Then, having rubbed it over
with butter, insert a mix of thyme sprigs or dried
thyme with grated nutmeg and salt into the slits. Grill
or barbeque the fish, basting it at intervals. Slices of
gammon could also be grilled or barbequed at the same
time and a gravy made by heating ¼ pint (150 ml) of
red wine, a few minced oysters and their liquor, 2 oz
(55 g) prawns and 2 hard boiled eggs. Modern cooks
may prefer to thicken the liquor as needed with a little
grated bread.

CR80

*Carbonado

45

To Force a Leg of Mutton.

Take a large leg of Mutton. Cut all ye meat out of ye skin, leaving ye skin whole. Then take ye meat, shreed it very smale with half a pound of suet. Then take two handfulls of sweet herbs as saige, Sweet Margerum & tyme, ye leafes of Sorell & Parsley ; shred all these amoungest your meat & season it with pepper & salt, Nutmeg according to your taste. Then take 4 egges & mix with your meat & put it into your skin, & lape it up in a cloath & let it boyle till it is enough. Serve it up with Caper sace, anchoveys, butter & Vineger with parcley boylet.

This recipe is self-explanatory.

CB80

To Preserve Barberryes in Jelly.

Take a pound of ye best Barberryes when they are ripe, stoned, & tye them up in bunches & put to them a pound & half of Double refined Suger beaten very fine, put them in to a silver bason, then pick a pint of barberyes & put to them a pint of barberrys water & give them one boyle till the skins are swelled. Then sqwees them gently tell you have a quarter of a pint of syrrup. Power this upon ye suger & barberryes, then set your bason upon a skillet of watter that boyles very fast, & so keep them boyling till ye barberryes look very cleare & shine & look of pure scarlet colwer. Then take out ye barberryes & put them up, & let ye syrrup stand ontill it be thick of a stife jelly. Then put it on your barberryes.

If you have barberries, the instructions above are clear, but remember once again that Lady Ann's pint is 16 fl oz (475 ml) only. Barberries are not commonly available among fruits on sale. The barberry is the red fruit of the Berberis vulgaris *and is a rather long oval in shape. Identify them carefully before using. You may find some growing wild but this is unlikely.* Berberis vulgaris *can be grown in the garden and the berries used to flavour meat during roasting, especially lamb. They can be candied, made into jelly, mixed with other fruits in preserves, or used to fill small tarts.*

∞

A quakin puding.

A pint of Creame & boyl in it a littel Mace; then take ye yolks of 3 egges & ye whites of 3 or 4 & put them into ye Cream & stir it till it is allmost cold. Then put in a spoonfull of flower & as much grated bread as will make it of ye thickness of butter. Put in a Nutmeg & a quarter of a pound of Suger; beat it very well & put it into Cloth well flowered & boyl it an hour. White Wine & butter & suger for ye juce.

Ingredients:

8 fl oz (240 ml) double cream
Pinch mace
2 small eggs
1 level tablespoon white SR flour

7 tablespoons brown breadcrumbs
¾ teaspoon grated nutmeg
1½ oz (45 g) golden caster sugar

Add the mace to the cream in a small pan and bring to the boil. Pour the cream into a bowl to cool and leave until is hand-hot. Meanwhile beat the eggs well. When the cream has cooled, stir in the beaten eggs and continue stirring until it is cold. Add the sieved flour, and then stir in the breadcrumbs gradually until it reaches a sauce consistency. (It needs to resemble butter that has not stood in the fridge, but that has not melted either.) Stir in the nutmeg and sugar. Pour into a wetted heatproof bowl or, if preferred, a floured cheesecloth or small jelly bag. Cover with a lid or double greaseproof paper with foil secured over, or tie with a strong thread as appropriate. Place in double pan or on trivet in pan of boiling water and boil for one hour.

CB&O

To Hash a Calve's Head.

Let your Calve's head be half boyled & cut it in small peces, toung & all; put it into a stupan; put to it a prettie deel of sallt and anchove pepper, Cloves, & a Oinon, a bundell of sweethearbes, and as much sider or white Wine & water as will cover it. Stu this till ye licker be half wasted, then put in 7 yolks of egges beaten with a spoonful of Viniger; put it in & stir it on ye fire till it is thick & sarve it up with ye brans fried & forsed Meat balls & slised Lemon.

> To Hash a Calve's Head and To Pickle Oysters are unlikely recipes for this day and age.

To Pickell Oysters.

Take one Gallon of rock Oysters with ye licqur, &
put them in a deep dish or bason with a pint of white
Wine Vinegare, & get them over ye fire till they
simmer, & when they boile take them off. Put in salt
to your taste a lettil before you take them off ye fire;
then take an Ounce & half of white pepper, 4 or 5
large blades of Mace, 10 or 12 Cloves, one Nutmeg
quarttered, a Lemon slised & a Oinon. Put all these
in your pot & put your Oisters into them & strane ye
Licquer over them. Next day take out ye Lemon &
Onion.

*This might be rather an expensive recipe to make
nowadays, but an interesting one.*

C3&O

For Honeycomb Cakes.

Take ye single leaves of Oranges flowers & boyl them
in a preaty Deall of Water till they look clear; then
put them into a Cloath to Dry. Beat your sugar very
fine & boil it to a candy. Then put in ye Orange
flowers. Have in readyness paper coffenss on a fin
plate. As soon as it comes to a candy again, hold ye
tin over a hot fire & fill in your candy into ye
coffinss till they boyl up to ye top. Then clap ye tin
down on a very wet cloth & when they are dry take
them out.

At the time of Lady Ann, orange trees were commonly grown in the bigger houses, and so the very strongly scented and flavoured flowers were readily available for this recipe.

CЗ⊗Ю

To make Allmand flumry.

Take a pint of strong jelley & a quarter of a pound of almands, blanched & beat very fine, with Orange flower watter. Then put them into a strainer & wash them through with hott jelly as clean as you can & sweten it to your taste with Double refind sugar & set it over ye fire & stir it till it is ready to boil. Then put it in dishes & turn it out when it is cold.

Ingredients:

5 medium apples
12 fl oz (360 ml) water
12 oz (325 g) golden caster sugar
1 dessertspoon orange-flower water
3-4 oz (80-100 g) ground almonds
Fingers of plain biscuit
Segments of orange

The jelly referred to here is made by washing and cutting the apples into four leaving the cores and peel. Place in a large pan, pour over water and partially cover. Boil until the apples are mushy. The apples and liquor are then poured into a jelly bag and hung over a large jug or bowl. When the apples have cooled it may be necessary to give them a gentle squeeze in order to obtain 14 fl oz (410 ml) of apple liquor. This is poured into a pan and the sugar melted in. Bring the liquor to the boil and boil rapidly for approximately 12 minutes, until the liquor forms a thick droplet on the edge of the spoon. Stand aside to cool for a minute or two. Stir in the orange-flower water. Put one-third of the almonds into a sieve and pour over a third of the hot apple jelly. Work both through the sieve together into a large jug. Repeat twice more until all the liquor and almonds are mixed in the jug. Stir and then pour into individual glass dishes. Serve garnished with fingers of plain biscuit and orange segments.

> *This is a tasty dish but is very sweet. It makes a useful topping for pears or tart fruits. Plain biscuit also complements the flavour. Biscuits made Mrs. B's way on page 32 will go very well. It will keep in the refrigerator.*

To Make Cowslip Wine. (Lady Powe)

To every gallon of water take 2 pounds of sugar & lett them boyle one Hour together. Scum it & stran it off; order it as you do wort; when it is cold enough, put to every gallon of water one spoon full of yeast & when it is a little white put it into your vessell & to every gallon put 6 or 7 quarts of picked cowslips & ye juce of 2 or 3 lemons & ye pell of some of them. The cowslips must be stirred 3 days befor you stop it close, & when it is stopped close let it stand 3 weeks or a month. Before you bottle it put in a lump of sugar. This is approv'd.

Cowslip has to be the most delicious wine to make, with a wonderful richness, quite bordering a liqueur without the high alcohol content. For centuries, cowslip was the favourite wine. Cowslips are now rare in the countryside and are consequently protected by law, but plants or seeds are available from catalogues and garden centres. Cowslips prefer a chalky soil and like to be mixed with other plants or in grassy areas. I have grown them successfully for wine making over many years.

In this recipe, the sugar can be added to the boiled water in the fermenting bin along with the cowslip flowers. I find 1½ - 2 pints (900-1200 ml) of flowers are sufficient to produce an excellent wine; you do not need the quantity given here. Amazing as the flavour must have been, it is not realistic for us to pick so many nowadays. Use one large or two small lemons. Baker's yeast set on toast can be floated on top for 24 hours after it has reached blood heat; once the yeast is removed, stir the wine in the fermenting bucket twice a day for about seven days, then put into a demijohn until it finishes working. *(For my own cowslip wine recipe see* Herb Sufficient *also published by Heartsease Books.)*

CR&

To make Goosberrys Vinegar.

When ye goosberrys are full ripe bruis them very well, & to every quart of Goosberrys when brused, put 3 quarts of water that has boyled well, & scumm'd, & is quite cold again. Let it stand mixed 24 hours, then stran it thro a flannel bag & to every gallon of liquor put a pound & a quarter of brown suger. Then barrel it up & stop it close: ye second year it will be fit for use.

Gooseberry vinegar, barberry drope's and potted tongue are unlikely recipes in a modern setting. I have explained about barberries on page 47.

CB80

To Make Barbary Drope's.

Take a good quantity of barbary's. Strip them of ye stalks & put to them a litle water to keep them from burning. Boyl them & mash them as they boyl; let them boyl till they are very deep coullered; rub them through a hair sieve, then stran them through a straner that there be none of ye black noses in them. Make them scalding hot, & to half a pint of ye jelley a pound of sifted suger, & let it scald, & drop it on bords or glasse's. Put them in a stove, & turn them when dry.

CB80

To Pott Tongues.

Take two Neats' Tongues cut off all ye root; salt them with two Oz of Salt Peter, & as much comon Salt as will cover them. Put them in a deep pott, that they may lye under the brine. You must salt & turn them every two Days till they are hard. Boyl & Blanch them. Season them with Pepper & Ginger, of each a quarter of a Oz & as much cloves & Mace together, two Nutmegs. Beat all well & rub over ye Tongues, put into ye pot 1/2 a pint of Water; lay them in Softly with all ye spice about them; put a pound of butter over them & lye a paper on ye pott & cover it with a course paste. Bake it with Household bread. When almost cold, take them out of ye pott & when quite cold cover them with Clarified Butter.

CR&O

Surfeit Water.

Take 5 Pints of Anniseed water, a peck of poppy flowers, 2 Oz of Liquorish, 1/2 a pound of Raisons of ye sun, 1/2 a pound of figgs, a quarter of an Oz of safron, 2 Oz of Anniseeds. Bruise ye Anniseeds, slice & scrape ye Liquorish, quarter ye figgs, stone ye raisons, pull ye safron with your fingers, put 1/2 a handfull of maryigolds to ye rest. Put them all into ye Anniseed water, ye Safron last, stir it every Day in ye form of a figure of 8. Then strain it into bottles, put ye Ingredients (when ye Water is strained off) into a cold still & still it off- Put it into bottles well cork'd.

This sounds good but cannot be made today.

CR&O

Fritters.

Take 11 eggs, & 9 of ye Yolks, beat them well & putt to them a pint of Cream. Mix it with ye finest flower about ye thickness of a pudding, & put to it salt, Nutmeg, Mace, & Cinamond a pretty deal, & beat it well together & let it stand 3 or 4 hours before you fry them, cover'd up before ye fire. Then pare 18 small pipins & slice them as thin as a Wafer. When you are ready to fry them add to your butter, sack, brandy, strong Ale, or beer, not bitter, of each 5 spoonfulls mixt together, & made scalding hot. Then put it into ye stiff bater & beat it well together. Let there be in ye stew-pan 2 pound of beef dripping & 2 pound of hogs Lard. When it boyles well up dip your slices into ye batter & put them quick into ye fat, & another must stand to turn & take them out, laying them on a hot coarse Cloth before ye fire till you have enough to send up. You will scarse complain of this quantity being too small, but 'tis just as it was given me in--- *(receipt stops here)*

Ingredients:

3 egg whites + 2 egg yolks
4 fl oz (120 ml) single cream
1½ teaspoons cinnamon
1 teaspoon nutmeg
½ teaspoon freshly ground mace
5 oz (150 g) sieved SR flour
1 dessertspoon each of sweet sherry and brandy (or ale could be used)

2 or 3 cooking apples
Butter or oil for frying.

Beat the egg yolks and whites well in a blender, then add the cream and mix again. Spoon in the flour and spices and blend. Leave to stand, covered, for a couple of hours.

When ready to cook the fritters, peel, core and slice the cooking apples. The slices must be thin enough to cook through in the time it takes to fry the batter covering. Add the sherry and brandy, or ale, to the batter and blend. Add the sliced apple and stir. Fry in butter or oil until browned. Set them on a dish and keep hot until all are cooked or, if you have an eager queue drawn by the delightful aroma of cooking, dish the fritters up straight from the pan.

These are quite delicious! The apple has not been sweetened; those with a sweet tooth may like a drizzled topping of syrup or a little dark brown sugar.

෴

To Make Veal Glew.

Take a Leg of Veal & when ye fat is cut clean off, make a very strong broth of it & strain it thro a fine sieve that it may be clear. When this is done put ye broth into a bread flat stew pan that will hold it all, & set it on a high Chaffindish of Charkcoal, & stir it continually about that it may neither burn nor boyl ye whole time 'tis on ye fire, which must be about seven hours. After you set it by in your pan for a day or two, then put it out & scrape off the

stettlement if any. Put ye clean jelly into a China
Dish & place it in a Stewpan of hot Water, placing it
on a Chaffin of Charkcoal; then ye hot water in ye
pan must be kept boyling, til by ye steam ye jelly
grow of a Glewish substance, which it will do in two
or three hours. -You may know when it is done
enough by putting a Little by to be cold, & if 'twill
cut like a soft cheese it is as it should be. – Put it into
little sweetmeat pots till it is quite cold; then you
may take it out & wrap it in flanell & afterward in
paper & it will keep many years. - A piece ye bigness
of a Nutmeg will make half a pint of broth. The
whole Leg of Veal, unless very large, will not make a
piece of Glew bigger than your hand. It is made
into broth by pouring hot Water on it.

*Veal Glew is not a likely recipe for the modern
kitchen.*

CB&O

Dry'd Cherrys.

Stone ye Cherrys when they are very fresh, & to five
pound of Cherrys (when ston'd) allow a pound of
fine powder sugar. Put ye Liquor that runs from ye
cherrys in ye Stoneing into ye bottom of your
preserving pan. Then Lay in ye Cherrys on ye
Sugar till all are in; then set them on a charkcoal
fire, not very quick, & as ye suggar melts & ye
Liquor encreases, make ye fire quicker & let them
jest scald. Then put them out into a earthen pan & set

them by for a day or 2; then scald them again; then drain them from ye Liquor & lay them on sieve & keep them turn'd till they are so dry as to rattle.

Ingredients:

2 lb (900 g) cherries –1¾ lb (800 g) when stoned
4 oz (120 g) golden caster sugar

Stone the fresh cherries over a bowl, so collecting any juice that runs from them as you do it. Discard the stones. Put the sugar in a pan and melt it over a low heat; as it melts add the cherries. If the cherries have not produced much juice you may need a little water (about a tablespoonful) in the bottom of the pan to stop the sugar from sticking. When the sugar has thoroughly melted, turn up the heat and bring to the boil. The pan should be on the heat for about 10 minutes before it comes to the boil. Keep the cherries boiling for just 1 minute, no longer – you do not want them to lose shape. Remove from the heat. Pour the cherries and liquor into a casserole dish and cover with a lid. Set the dish aside for two days.

Return the cherries and liquor to a pan and bring to the boil once more. Strain out the cherries with a slotted spoon and lay them on a sieve to drain. Once fully drained they can be set on a fine cake rack or on muslin over a tray, in a warm place — either in a top oven when the bottom oven is in use, in the sun with a fly cover or with the oven cooling at below 100°C. They need to be dried until they would rattle if placed on a metal surface or tin. They can then be stored in jars and used in cakes and puddings.

It is surprising how much of the cherry flavour survives. These are still good to eat as healthy sweets months later and, although preserved, they are neither sugary nor dry.

CROSS

To Make Gravysoop.
(from Serjeants' Inn* Cook)

Have a good strong broth made of a Legg of beef & seson'd with time & Cloves & mace, & when 'tis well boyld, that you think it will jelly when 'tis cold, strain it off ye broth from ye meat. Then put your broth into a pot that you design to make your soop in & have in readiness these soop hearbs, viz. some Sallery & judiss & spinidge. Clean them & chop them small, & stew them well in a stew pan over a clear fire. Then put them into your broth & let them boyl gently, & some Oxes pallets, & let them be boyl'd very tender & cut them in very small slices. Then put them into your soop, & Season it with peper & salt & Nutmeg to your pallet, & dish it up with a Roasted duck or fowl in ye middle & dry some french bread & break it into your soop.

So serve it up to Table.

*Before he was made a judge and knighted Ann's husband was styled 'Mr Serjeant Blencowe' and was a member of the Inner Temple, one of the four 'Inns of Court': Lincoln's Inn, Gray's Inn, the Middle Temple and the Inner Temple. Did he bring this recipe home after enjoying a dinner at the Inner Temple or did his wife dine there as a guest?

It is unusual in this century to use meat stocks as the basis for soups, although only fifty years ago this would have struck a much more familiar chord to cooks. Nor are ox's pallets considered a delicacy any longer. However, for anyone who fancies experimenting using a meat stock spiced with cloves and mace, and then adding celery and spinach this could be an interesting recipe to try.

CR&O

A Good Potatoe pudding, ye best.

Take a pound of potatoes, boyl'd, peel'd & cold, mash them thro a strainer. Then add one pound of fresh butter melted, 10 Eggs, ½ pound of suggar, ½ a Nutmeg : mix these together & put it in a quick Oven. One hour will bake it.

Ingredients:

9 oz (255 g) cooked potatoes
1 oz (30 g) golden caster sugar
5 eggs
6 oz (170 g) melted butter
1 teaspoon grated nutmeg

Put the cooked potatoes into a mixer or blender and mash until they resemble a smooth cold paste. Add the sugar and well-beaten eggs. When all this is well combined, with the mixer on slow, pour the melted butter slowly in at the side of the bowl. Add the nutmeg and stir. Bake in a deep casserole dish at 160°C in a fan-assisted oven. Serve immediately.

This is really almost a potato soufflé, tasting rather like sweet potatoes. It is especially good served with fish or chicken. The sugar is reduced for modern taste.

CR80

A Receipt to preserve Peaches in Brandy.

The peaches must be ripe, but not too ripe. You must put them in boyling water in order to peel them, & let them continue there till you find ye skins will easily come off. Which when you have done, fling them instantly into fresh water, & when you take them out of that, then put them into clarifi'd sugar &.give them one Boyling, & so let them cool in ye sugar, that it may soak well into them, & then put them upon a sieve or a plate with holes & then reboyl ye sugar till it will stick to your finger. Repeat this method 3 times, both in relation to ye peaches & sugar, after which ye Peaches so prepar'd must be put into glass bottles, which are to be fill 'd after this manner; half Brandy, half ye sirrup made by ye boyling ye peaches in ye sugar; & so they are to be kept for use. The same way will do for Peaches, & Admirable Plums.

Ingredients (To make one large and one small jar):

2 lb (900 g) peaches
1 lb (455 g) white granulated sugar
Brandy

Use firm, ripe-looking peaches. In order to peel them easily, cover them in boiling water in a pan and set over a moderate heat for a few minutes. Check after 5 minutes, turning them. Peel the skin away as soon as they are come away easily and place each in a jug of cold water as soon as it is peeled.

Put half the sugar into a large pan and then lay the whole peaches on top and cover with the remainder of the sugar. Leave to stand with the lid on for about 10 minutes, by which time the sugar should have dissolved. Set the pan over a low to moderate heat and bring to a fast boil, turning the fruit gently. As soon as it reaches a fast boil, place the lid on the pan and remove from the heat to cool and for the fruit to soak up the syrup. Turn the fruit once after 10 minutes in order to coat them with the syrup.

Remove the peaches with a slotted spoon, first onto a sieve and then onto a plate. Return to the pan any syrup that has drained from the sieve and bring the syrup back to the boil. Boil for about 5 minutes until a little on a saucer will stick to your finger when slightly cooled. When this point is reached you will notice a change in the syrup: it will appear thicker in the bottom of the pan.

Put the peaches back into the syrup and bring to the boil, coating them with the syrup as you do so. Before you take them out of the pan turn them for a full coating. Stand the pan away from the stove with the lid on to cool for 10 minutes. Turn the peaches in the syrup again and repeat as above, twice.

Finally, spoon the peaches into jars with screw-top or

airtight lids, and cover half in the syrup and half in brandy.

This method may be time consuming, but what you are doing is allowing liquor coming out of the peaches to be boiled off and steadily replacing it with the sugar syrup. The result is amazing, a truly elegant preserve fit for a very special occasion.

To Make Caramell.

Take China Oranges, peel them & split them in quarters, but dont break ye skin. Lay ye Quarters before ye fire; turn them till ye skin is very dry ; then take half a pound of fine sugar sifted thro a hair sieve, put it in a brass or silver pan, set it over a slow fire & keep it stirring till it is melted & looks pretty clear. Then take it off ye fire & put in ye Orange Quarters ; put one at a time ; take it out again as fast as you can with a silver spoon & lay them on a dish, which you must butter or it will not come off ; ye sugar will keep hot enough to do any plate full. You may do roasted Chesnuts ye same way, or any fruit in ye sumer, but first lay ye fruit before ye fire or in a stove to make ye skin tuff. If any wet comes out ye suggar will not stick to it ; it must be done just when you use it : it will not keep.

This is simply dipping portions of oranges or chestnuts in a sugar coating. Since Lady Ann warns that the finished item will not keep, there is no intention to candy the fruit.

To make Beef à la mode.

Take a fine sir Loyn of Beef, & bone it & take ye fillit
out of it; & then take ye Back of ye sir Loyn & lard it
with large larding bacon, very thick, thro' & thro'.
Then take your Beef & put it in a large pan as will
hold gravy enough to stew it in, & let your gravy be
very brown : then put your Beef in ye Oven pretty Hot.
In ye baking of it turn it upside down once or twice, & let
it bake 2 or 3 hours, according as it is in bigness, till
'tis tender. Then make a fine brown Raggooe of what
you please in it, as Cox Combs — pallates,
mushrooms, morrells, forc't Balls, Sweet Breads,
&ca. Then take your Beef out of ye Oven, just as you
are ready to dish it up, & then take ye sir Loyn & let
it be dish'd up hot with ye Raggooe about it well
relish'd.

For the 21st Century taste, this recipe could be
made without the cocks combs and palates. The
London Art of Cookery, published in 1807, contains a chapter on 'Ragoos' and gives a beef recipe
also containing mushrooms and morels, with the
instructions: "If you please you may add a
sweetbread cut in six pieces, a palate stewed tender
and cut into little pieces, some cocks-combs, and a
few forcemeat balls. Though these are great
additions, yet it will do very well without them."
The 1807 recipe suggests adding instead a large
bunch of celery chopped, 2 spoonfuls of ketchup and
a glass of red wine.

CʒꙄ

To dry Apricotts like prunelloes.

Take a pound of Apricotts, stone them, pare them &
strew a quarter of a pound of beaten sugar over &
under them. When 'tis dissolv'd set it over a slow fire
to boyl: as they begin to boil, scum & turn them; if
any begin to break take them out till ye rest are
enough, then put them into syrup again: ye next
day heat them again, & let them stand 48 hours,
always cover'd, then heat them once more & set them
to dry on a sieve that ye syrup may run from them.
Then crack ye stones & blanch them & put them in.
And then put them into a stove or oven that is but
warm. Turn them on plates till they are as dry as
prunelloes, then dip a cloth in warm water & pott
them with it, that they may not be clammy, & then
dry them again a little. Between every row you put
into your gallipots, put a paper dip't in water & clapt
dry again, & tye them down close with dry paper.
Keep them in a place that's dry but not hot.

Ingredients:

1 lb (450 g) fresh apricots
4 oz (120 g) golden caster sugar

Put 2 oz (55 g) sugar into the bottom of a thick-
bottomed pan. Stone and peel the apricots, set them on
the sugar and pour the remainder of the sugar over. Set
the pan over a low heat for the sugar to dissolve – this
should take no more than 10 minutes. (Note, you do
not need to scum the liquor, something that was necessary in Lady Ann's day to remove impurities from the

sugar.) Turn up the heat to bring to the boil for no more than a minute. Small apricot halves will begin to break up quite quickly and you should remove them as soon as they do. Put the apricots into a casserole dish and pour the syrup over. Leave covered with a lid until the next day. Heat the fruit in the syrup until the syrup comes just to the boil. Pour back into the casserole dish and stand again for 48 hours.

Heat the apricots again in the syrup, bringing it just to the boil and then set the drained apricot halves onto a fine cake rack, or clean muslin set over one. Drip for 1 hour, turning them once. The stones need not be added. Then set the fruit onto plates in a warm place such as a top oven when the bottom oven is in use. After a couple of hours turn the fruit over, setting them on a fresh plate. When most of the syrup has gone, lay the apricots on a clean, damp cloth (dampness stops the apricots from sticking to the cloth) and pat them dry. This is to remove any excess syrup before final drying.

Return to a plate for a last stand in a warm place. They are ready when they resemble the plumped 'ready-to-eat' apricots sold now in vacuum packs.

This recipe is actually less of a trouble than it looks. It takes just a few minutes on several days. The result, in my opinion, is superior to any kind of dried apricots I have tasted before. Not only are they plump but also delicious and contain only a little added sweetening rather than modern chemicals to preserve them.

CB80

Hodg Podg

To 8 quarts of Water put a Pound of Beef or Mutton. Let it Boil gently & put in 4 Onions, a few sweet Hurbs, a Blade of Mace & a few cloves; then take 4 Turneps cut in slices & fry them brown; then take a little spinnage boil'd by it self, thin chopt, & a bunch of salary which should be boil'd in ye Broth, Chop that allso. When you dish it up first, take a bit of Butter & Brown it with a little flower, then put to it a Crust of White Bread, then put in ye meat & liquor & keep it over a gentle fire. Then put in ye Herbs & Turneps & garnish ye Dish with some of ye Turneps.

> *The title of this recipe can be found in numerous historical cookery books and the ingredients may vary considerably. This version uses rather a lot of water and turnip to a small amount of meat and other ingredients. The main difficulty with cooking this today is the size of pan needed. A cauldron would do well.*

CBEO

Butter'd Orange.

Cut ye yallow'd Rind of 2 Sevill Oranges into half a Pint of Spring Water & let them steep one Hower. Then strayn it & putt to ye liquor a pint of juce of Sevill Orange, & 6 eggs well beaten, & 6 Ounces of fine sugger. Then strain it again & put in 2 oz of Orange Peele, boil'd till ye bitterness be off, & then beat it fine, & 2 oz of Suger Bisket & a little

candied Orange Peell shreed. Set it over your fire &
stir it till 'tis thick; then putt in a little good Butter
& when 'tis as as you like, lay it in a heap in a Dish,
& garnish it with bits of savoy Bisket and Candied
Orange.

Ingredients:

Rind of 1 or 2 oranges
4 fl oz (120 ml) water
8 fl oz (240 ml) orange juice
3 beaten eggs
3 oz (85 g) sugar
2 oz (55 g) sweet biscuit
A little candied orange peel
Serves 3

Pare the rind very thinly from the orange, leaving the
white pith. Put the rind into the 4 fl oz (120 ml) water
and steep for 1 hour. Then strain, keeping the liquor as
you will add the eggs and sugar to this later. Put the
rind into a pan and cover well with fresh water. Boil
rapidly, partly covered, until the rind is no longer bitter, about one hour. Add more water as necessary.
Throw this water away.

  When the rind is ready, take the liquor you have kept
to one side and add the freshly squeezed and strained
orange juice (if you have only one orange this can be
topped up with pure orange juice from a carton). Put
the eggs and the sugar into a blender. Blend. Add the
orange juice and liquor and blend again. Grind the
boiled rind until it is fine, or chop. Add this with the
crumbled sweet biscuit and shredded candied peel and
blend. Pour all into a bowl set over a pan of boiling

water, stirring occasionally and then continuously as it comes to a thick custard consistency. Add a small knob of butter and stir in, then spoon into one or individual dishes and serve garnished with candied orange and/or pieces of sweet biscuit.

Oranges were very popular amongst those who could afford them at this period. This is a very tasty, smooth dessert that can be made early when entertaining. If you would like a stronger orange flavour boil the rind of two oranges, and add that of the second with the biscuit and candied peel.

CR&O

To make Shrub.

6 doz of Lemons, a Doz of Oranges, 6 Pounds of Sugar, & 12 bottles of Brandy. The Rine thinly Pared of one 3d of ye Lemons and Oranges, laid 12 hours in 2 bottles of ye Brandy. The Rinds thrown away & ye Juce of ye Lemons & Oranges being strain'd very fine throu a jelly Bagg and ye Suggar dissolved. Put it into a Cask till very fine, which may be 3, 4, or 5 months, then bottle it for use.

N.B.-Three pints of Hot or Cold water put to a Bottle of ye foregoing composition will make good Punch and, taken solely, a Pleasant Dram.

Ingredients:

2 bottles brandy
12 lemons
1 orange

1 lb (450 g) light brown soft sugar
Rind from 4 lemons and from one-third of an orange

In the evening of the first day, pare the rind thinly, leaving the white pith on the fruit. Add this to the brandy, sharing it between the two bottles. Leave for 12 hours. Next morning, strain the juice from the lemons and orange through a fine nylon sieve. Crush any lumps in the sugar before stirring into the juices and adding the brandy. Stir to be sure the sugar is completely dissolved. Pour into bottles; you will now need a third bottle to take the amount.

CX8O

To make Lemon Sillibubes.

Take a quart of Cream, 3 quarters of a pound of double refine sugar, & ye juce of 4 lemons with some of ye peel grated into a pint of white wine, and half a pint of sack. Put all these into a clean pan & with a wisk keep it stirring all one way for half an hour. Then take off ye froth as it rises & put into your glasses: it is the better for keeping two or three days & will keep a week.

Ingredients:

8 fl oz (240 ml) double cream
3 oz (85 g) golden caster sugar
Juice of a lemon
4 fl oz (120 ml) white wine
2 fl oz (60 ml) medium or sweet sherry
Serves four

Add the lemon juice to the sugar and mix well. Add the sherry and wine and blend in, then add the cream still stirring or mixing. This is best done in a blender. When the froth rises, stop mixing and spoon the froth into sundae dishes. Blend again and repeat until there is little left in the blender. Pour the remainder slowly into the glasses at the sides so as not to disturb the froth. Can be eaten immediately or kept in the fridge for one or two days.

The wine and sherry act as preservatives. This is a rather alcoholic and very elegant dish, suitable for special occasions.

CB80

To make minc'd pyes

Take a Large Neat's tongue and boyl it till 'twill peel. When peeled, cut all that is fitt for use into thin slices, weigh it & take half as much more fresh Beaf suitt; shred your meat small and mix your suet with it; mix both together as small as possible; put to it a pound of raisons of ye sun, ston'd, five hard pipins, ye rind of a Lemman, & ye Rind of a sevil orange shred very small. Shred too yuor Raisons & pippens amongst ye meat. Mix all this well together, and put into them Two nutmegs, some sinemone, mace, & a few cloves, all finly beaten, a quarter of a pint of sack, a little salt, & three quarters of a pound of suger, some Canded Cylon Lemon & oringe peell cut into thin slices, three pounds of courants cleen pick't, wash't, and dry'd, & ye Juce of four Lemons.

This is a typical early recipe for mince pies. How they have changed! With the quantities drastically reduced, perhaps using a small tin of tongue, this recipe could make your mince pies a real talking point at Christmas.

To do green oranges.
(Lady Stapleton's way)

Lay them in salt & water for nine days, shifting the water. Then boil them till there clear, in water, & drain them clean from that, & then putting them in a cold surrup, & keep them for use & put them in apple jelly as you please. You may do ripe oranges the same way. When they are boil'd, let them be cover'd close.

This recipe reminds us once again that oranges were grown as part of the home fruit supply. Just as we might need recipes to take care of green tomatoes, Lady Ann might need a recipe for a surfeit of green oranges.

To Do hartichock bottoms.

Cut all the leaves & chock off, & sok them in cold water. Then change the water once or twice, & after that stew them in a little water with gravey & butter, & serve them up so : or fry them, which you please.

Artichokes were very popular and this recipe simply describes how Lady Ann prepared and cooked them.

CB80

To Roast Fowls (or ducks) (Sir Thomas Perkingses way)

You may Roast the Fowl with about fifteen middling sizd raw Oysters in each Fowl, with a Scotch Onion, or two, according to the size of the Fowl, which Onions must be taken out when you Cut up the Fowl. Run two or three spoonfull of Cloves thro them when drawn in the dish. Rost them by a brisk Fire even to Crisp ye feet, which must be laid flatt backwards towards the rump for their being Easier carv'd; but roast not the bodyes of the Fowl too much, that the gravey may be in them, and if they be under done you may mend them by stewing. Don't spit them upon a great spit, which will let their Gravey out, but upon Iron skewers, on which tye them back to back fast on your Spitt.

This recipe gives us a very clear picture of roasting in the great hearth of the kitchen,

CB80

To Make a Delma.

Take the Lean meat of a Loyn of mutton and as much beef Suet, shread it small as for force meat. Then put the same quantity of Rice boyld tender, season it with sweet herbs, salt & pepper, & a little nutmeg; then mix it all together and brake in one or two eggs according to the quantity of your meat. Then take Cabbage or vine leaves and dip them in hot water, then role the meat in ye leaves about the bigness of a small Cucumber, and tye them with course thread, put them into a stewpan with gravey, put them over a gentle fire cover'd. Lett them stew till they are thoroughly done, then take them out and take off the thread, thicken the gravey with the yolk of an egg and pour it over your meat.

Ingredients:

4 oz (120 g) long grain rice
1 teaspoon dried marjoram
1 teaspoon dried thyme
1 teaspoon dried parsley
½ teaspoon of savory   Freshly grated nutmeg
12 oz (340 g) lean, minced, lamb
2 oz (55 g) beef suet (**or** 2 oz (55 g) beef fat)
1 egg
Savoy cabbage **or** tinned vine leaves
Stock cube & water

Boil the rice in water until tender, drain and season with the herbs, salt and pepper to taste and a little freshly grated nutmeg. Mix the seasoned rice with the meat and chopped suet or fat. Add sufficient beaten egg to mix. Form into approximately 6 rolls, the thickness of a small cucumber each, to fit the leaves. Then take the cabbage or vine leaves and dip them in hot water before laying them on a board. Place a roll of meat mix on the centre of each leaf and wrap the leaf around it. Tie a strong thread around the rolls in two places to hold them closed and put them into stock (deep enough to half cover them), in a large covered pan. Bring to boil and keep on a low heat for about an hour. Lift out the cooked Delmas and keep these hot while you thicken the gravy by stirring in a beaten egg yolk if desired. Do not forget to remove the ties before serving.

This dish may take time to cook, but is easy to make and very tasty. Beef suet is traditionally fat from the kidney of the animal rather than from other parts, but alternative fats go well. The amount of fat used can be altered to your taste — you will see I have already considerably reduced it from the original.

When mutton was used, this would have enriched the flavour. In this way, the Delma meets Lady Ann's consistent standards of elegant presentation and good flavour.

⊂ℬ℘

A Rabit Pye. (Mrs. Sydall)

Truse two small Rabits with there heads on, and turn'd to the middle of ther backs. Then Season 'em with pepper & salt & put 'em in a Pye, raised oval or square. Then put to 'em a little strong broth & a little butter & close your Pye & bake it; & against it comes out of the oven, have redy made a Ragoo, brown, with butter and flower (a little brown only) & good Gravy & Morells & trufells & mushrooms and Cocks Combs & Pallets & sweetbreads & Asparagus topps boyld tender, & put to 'em a little Melted butter. Shake these well together & poure it in our Pan & Garnish with ye Lidd Cutt & Serve it hott.

> *Mrs. Sydall's Rabbit Pie is an unlikely dish for the modern cook; however, the instructions are clear for anyone wishing to try it. The Ragoo could be altered as in Beef à la mode on page 64.*

❦

To Dobe a Rump of Beef. (Mrs. Sydall)

Bone your Beef & Lard it through with fatt Bacon about ye size of your little finger. Dip the Bacon first in juice steept in vinagar, then brown the Beef with butter, of a fine Brown; then put it in a pott with all the Gravy & Butter 'twas brownd in, & putt to it a pint of port wine, & sharp'n it with vinegar to your taste & season it with pepper and Salt & all spice (but don't put in much spice), & some onions stuck with cloves, & a bundle of parsly & Time & margrum &

Green Salery, or blanch'd as you can have it, &
Carots & Parsnips & Turnips in the time of year.
Cover it close & keep it scum'd between whiles, & let it
stew three or four hours. Then make a Raggo with
brown butter & flower & some of Ye Gravy that ye
meat was stew'd in: but you must first put to it a
little other Drawn Gravy, & only put in a little of
that ye meat was stewd in to sharp'n it: and put into
your Ragoo, Salery Cut, & hartichoke bottoms boyld
tender & cut like dice, & Potatoes & turneps & carots &
parsnips, all of 'em boyld tender & Cut in Bitts & a
heele sweetbreed boyld & cut in Dice, & forc't meat
balls boyld; Morells & Trufells if you pleass; shake
these well in your Ragoo & pour it on & round your
Beef Garnish with Lemon, &c.

The London Art of Cookery (1807) contains a
recipe very similar to this, evidently it continued to
be popular.

03&0

An Oyster Pye. (Mrs. Sydall)

Take about a quart of oysters & take off ye black
fins, & wash 'em clean & blanch 'em & Drayn the
Liquor from them; then take a quarter of a pound of
fresh butter & a minced anchovie & two spoonfulls of
Grated bread, & a spoonfull of minced Parsly, & a
little pepper, & a little grated Nuttmeg, no Salt (for
ye anchovie is salt enough). Squese these into a
lump, then line your Patepan with good cold crust,

77

but not flacky, and put one half of your mix'd Butter & anchovie &c. at the bottom; then lay your oysters, two or three thick at most; then put 'em ye other half of mixed Butter & anchovie &c. pick some grayns of Lemon on ye top (& some youlks of hard egg if you like 'em).   Put in 2 or 3 spoonfulls of ye oyster liquor and close it with ye Crust which should be a good deal higher then ye oysters to keep in the Liquor. Bake it, & when it comes out of the oven cut up the Lid, and have ready a little oyster Lyquor & Lemon juce stew'd togather, & pour it in & cut ye lidd in Peices & lay round it.

Another clear recipe.

ᘓ𝄞ᘔ

Mrs. Tashis little Puddings.

To nine eggs put a pint of Cream, & mix it pretty stiff with flower; put in 3 spoonfuls of yeast; & then let it stand two hours by the fire to rise; Grate in the Peel of one Lemmon & some suger. Put it into Tins. A quarter of an hour will bake them; if you pleas, you may put in a little Lemon juice.

Ingredients:

3 eggs
5 generous fl oz (150 ml) double cream
1 tablespoon fresh baker's yeast
1½ teaspoons grated lemon peel
5 oz (140 g) SR flour, either white or half white and half wholemeal

Petty Pattys with salad, dish of Pickle Lila and a goblet of Sage Wine.

Below- Salted vegetables and plums, preparing Pickle Lila.

Heating the peaches in syrup ready for preserving in brandy.

Left- Preparing the pastry covering for Bombard Apples.

Cowslip Wine, Ratafia
biscuits and Spanish
Custard decorated with
Gingerbread.

Below- Potato Pudding
and Dolmas, a flask of
Sage Wine behind.

Lady Anne Blencowe.

Buns, Marston Way from the oven.
Courtesy Weald and Downland Open Air Museum.

Brandy Cake, Lemon Sillabubs and Almond Flummery.

Below- Tansy Pudding, Mrs. Harvey's Pancakes, with Lemons in Segments and Dried Cherries.

Mrs. Tashis Little
Puddings, Apricot and
Cherry Preserves behind.
Ratafia biscuits and Clear
Jelly foreground.

Right- Potted Beef.

Herbal roots, resins and petal ingredients for the Physical recipes.
Alembic for distilling behind.

2 oz (55 g) + 2 teaspoons golden caster sugar
2 teaspoons lemon juice (optional)
Serves 6-8

Pour 2 fl oz (60 ml) of the cream into a warmed jug, add the crushed yeast and the 2 teaspoons of sugar. Stir and set in a warm place until frothy and risen (about 10 minutes). Break the eggs into a blender and add the remainder of the cream. Blend. Continuing to blend, add the sieved flour gradually. Pour into a warmed bowl. When the yeast mix is ready, stir into the mixture, cover with a damp cloth and set in a warm place to rise for one hour. By this time it should have doubled in size.

Add the grated lemon peel to the remainder of the sugar and warm before adding. Stir well into the mix, adding 2 teaspoons of lemon juice if liked. Set to rise a second time.

After approximately half an hour, spoon the mix into greased ramekin dishes. These should be half filled. Set to bake at 160°C (fan-assisted oven) for 15 minutes. Serve hot or cold with a fruit topping, with or without cream.

The method differs slightly from Lady Ann's original as we are not using ale yeast – this would already be working with sugar present. If made with white flour, the little puddings are similar to éclairs. They are quite delicious without being sweet. Making them with part wholemeal flour is healthier and still has tasters coming back for more.

CB&O

To make Cowslip Wine.

To every Gallon of Watter put two pounds of Loaf Sugar. Let it boyl an hour and strain it as you do Wort. When cold enough, put a little yest into it, and when it hath gathered to a Whitehead, put into it five Quarts of Coweslips picked, & the juice of two or three Lemmons, and the Peel of one. Stir it well togather and stop ye vessell close, and let it stand three weeks or a month. Then Bottle it. Let your vessell be too bigg by two or 3 gallons, or it will work over. Full half a pint of yest to fifteen Gallons.

That there is a second cowslip wine recipe is no surprise. Cowslip certainly appears to have been the favourite wine over centuries – and for good reason. I have even seen a recipe entitled "Cowslip wine made with plums" in an 18th century recipe book. It was really plum wine but clearly the writer felt a wine needed to be linked with cowslips. See the comments for Cowslip Wine on page 52.

See the comments for Cowslip Wine on page 52.

CঙৎᎶ

To Make Currant Wine (Mrs Durhame)

To a Bushal of Currants full ripe and strip'd, but pick'd clean from the leaves, put two Gallons of watter. Let it infuse a day or two, then strain it off, & to every gallon of Liquor put three pound & a half of suger. Then Tun it up, but not stop it close till it has done fermenting. Bottle it when 'tis fine, which may be in three months.

Again we find a great deal of fruit to 2 gallons (9 litres) of water, with half the amount of sugar to the gallon that we would mostly use. However, the currants are adding their own sugar.

☙❦

To Make Malena. (Mrs. Durhame)

Take twelve pound of Raisins of ye sun, chopt small, & boil three gallons of Spring water an hour, put it warm to ye Raisins & stir them well twice a Day for five days. Then put twelve pound of Honey to two gallons of Springwater when 'tis hot, & let it boil half an hour & scum it well, & stand in an earthen pot or Jar two days in a cool place. If made in ye Summer, press ye Raisins dry &.put both ye Liquors together & run 'em thro a Flannel Bag, & tun it in a wine vessel; & to ev'ry three gallons put an Ounce of Apricock Kernels cut small or beat, hang them in a bag in ye vessel, being unstop'd, for ten days; when it has done fermenting Stop it up for a Year.

I have yet to try this recipe.

81

To Make Raisin Wine.
(Mrs. Shurllock)

Take 3 qrts of a hundred of Raisins. Put them into a half Hogshead and fill it up with Water. Lett it stand open till the wine has done working. Then stop it up: it will be fine in 4 or 5 Months. River water is the best, and you must put it in cold. Mrs. Shurlock thinks Raisins of the Sun make the best Wine.

> *It seems this must have been popular by the amounts of ingredients. Half a hogshead as a wine measure is thirty one and a half gallons. I do not think health and safety would be happy with the river water used in this way!*

03℘

To Make Foule Brauth (Ann Sanders)

Take a Large foule & cut it in lems, & put it in a gallon of water, a pound or two of a Crage of Vell, a bunch of sweet earbes, & some Black pepper & mace. Let it boyle gentely 4 or 5 hours till it is all boyl'd to peeces. Then strane it through a seve; then put in 2 spoonfulls of Varmagely or Saggo, sume Blanched sallerrey & a lettes cutt in; if it is not theeck enough put in a little butter & flower Braded. Let it boyl up a lettle & then dish it up; some put in a Role Sliced; you must put in now Time; but a bay Lefe or 2 gives it a pretty flaver.

> *Varmagely is vermicelli.*

To Make ye best Clary Wine
(Miss Lyttelton)

Take four Gallons of Water, & when well boiled pour
it on twenty pound of Malego Raisons Clean Pick't &
chopt Small. Lett them Stand in the water nine
days, stirring them twice a day. Then strain them
thro a sive & squeese them dry with your Hands. Put
a Peck of Clary Flowers in your vessell, & pour ye
Liquor on them; stop it up for a fortnight, then draw
it into another vessell & let it stand till 'tis fine, &
then bottle it.

N.B. When you wrack it, put in half a Pound of Fine
Loaf Sugar.

> *The wild clary sage (Salvia verbenaca) is the clary
> referred to here. It has been a very popular wine in
> the past and still appeared in books on home wine
> making in the past sixty years.*

CƷ℥

White Scotch Collops (Lady Clarke)

Cut your veale thin, and hack it well with a roleing
pin, then beat up the youlks of three or four Eggs,
and dip every peice in. Then have ready your Stew -
pan with a peice of butter in it, and put them into it
to fry. You must put one Onion into the butter whole
before you put in the meat; when they are fryed
enough, which they will Soon be, for if they are long
a-doeing they turn brown, then put in one Anchovey;

when that is melted, put in Some Cream, which must be proportioned according to the quantity you make, and role some butter in some flowr and thicken it up & serve it.

This recipe is self-explanatory.

CB80

To make Petty Pattys
(Mrs. Barnardiston*)

Take the breast of a fowl or Turkey, mince it very fine, with the marrow of one bone, a few Crumbs of bread, a little Parcely and thime, some peper & salt, & a little onion. Mix all these together with an Egg as for forst meat, then bake them in the smallest patty pans you have, in puff paste, & before you send them to Table cut the tops off, and put in a little gravy. To be eat hot.

Ingredients:

12 oz (340 g) minced turkey breast
3 small slices brown bread
1 teaspoon of fresh or ½ teaspoon dried thyme
1 teaspoon fresh chopped parsley
½ medium onion
2 eggs
1 lb (450 g) puff pastry

*Lady Ann's grand-daughter Mary Jennens married Arthur Barnardistion, 'a wealthy trader in the Levant' with extensive property in Suffolk, in 1731. This was long after Ann's death, but it looks as if there had been a much earlier acquaintance between the families.

Mix the meat, breadcrumbs, herbs and finely chopped onion together; season with salt and pepper. Beat the eggs and add sufficient to bind the ingredients together. Save a little to paint onto the pastry case before it goes into the oven.

Roll out the puff pastry and line small bun tins or a larger dish, leaving sufficient to lay over the top. Fill the pastry cases and seal the puff pastry lids with the egg you have set on one side. Paint the top of each patty with egg and cook at 170°C for 40-50 minutes in a fan-assisted oven. Following Mrs. Barnidston's instruction, remove the lids just before serving and pour in a little gravy.

These are very tasty and suitable for serving for a light meal with salad.

CR80

To Pickle Lila, an Indian Pickle (Lord Kilmory)

Take of Ginger one pound; let it lye in salt and water one night. Scrape it and cut it in thin slices, & put it in a bottle with dry salt, and so let it remain till the rest of the ingredians are ready. Take Garlick one pound, peal of ye skins and salt it three days; then wash it & salt it again, & let it lye three days longer. Then wash it & put it upon a wooden seive to dry in the Sun. Take Cabbages cut, cut them in quarters and salt them & let them lye to dry in ye sun; so do Collyflowers & Sallery, cutting your Sallery as far as ye white is good, not thro the stalks; Redishes may be done the same way, only scraping them & leaving on ye tender tops; the Water must be all squesed out of ye Cabbages; french Beans & Asparagus, salted but two days, must have a boyl in salt & water, then be dryed in the sun. Take long Pepper, salt it and dry it, but not too much.. Take Mustard seed brused & Turmarick very fine. Put all the above ingredian into an Earthen pot, & if you would have it strong, put one Quart of strong Vinegar to three Quarts of stall; fill your Pot three quarters full; & then fill it up, & a fortnight after look at it. Then fill it again if there be occasion. After the same manner you may order Melons, or Cucumbers, Plums, or whatever you like this Pickle with. Half the Quantity of Garlick will do very well.

Ingredients:

2 oz (55 g) fresh garlic cloves
2oz (55g) shallots (optional)
4 oz (120 g) fresh root ginger
1 lb (450 g) coarse bay salt (or sea salt)
1 cabbage
Quarter of a cauliflower
4 large radishes
6-8 plums
¼ - ½ cucumber
6 (approx) French beans
2 pints (1.2 litres) distilled malt vinegar
1 oz (25 g) turmeric
4 oz (120 g) mustard seed
½ oz (15 g) whole white peppercorns
Preserving jar(s) with airtight seal(s)

Day 1. Take the garlic and peel each clove, cutting each one open at the top and bottom as you do so. Peel shallots, if using, and cut each one open at the top and bottom. Pack garlic and shallots in salt in a small covered dish or jar. Put whole fresh pieces of ginger into salt water.

Day 2. Strain the ginger pieces, scrape off the peel. Slice the ginger and put in a jar layered with salt. The first and last layers should be salt so that all the ginger is covered.

Day 4. Wash the garlic and shallots in cold water, dry using kitchen paper towel and put in a covered pot layered with salt, as described for the ginger.

Day 6. Cut a small cabbage into quarters, pouring salt in between the leaves and over the outer parts. Cut a quarter of a cauliflower into florets and salt these. Also scrape the skin off 4 large radishes, leaving them whole and salt them. Set all the salted vegetables on a cake rack and cover with a mesh cover to guard against flies. Leave in a sunny place in the kitchen to dry for 3 days, turning the vegetables at regular intervals.

Day 7. Wash the garlic and shallots again, then lay in the sun to dry with the vegetables.

Salt halved, stoned plums and thick slices of cucumber, setting these to dry with the other vegetables.

Day 9. Put the turmeric into a little of the cold vinegar. Mix. Bruise the mustard seed and peppercorns and add to the rest of the vinegar. Next add the ginger (having scraped away the salt from the pieces) and stir into the turmeric paste.

Pour sufficient water into a pan to cover all of the salted vegetables, then add salt to the water and stir until an egg will float in it (this takes a substantial amount of salt). Bring to the boil, add all the vegetables and boil for 1 minute. Drain them.

Bring the vinegar and spice mix to the boil and remove from the heat. Pack the drained vegetables and garlic (with the salt scraped away) into the jar or jars. Pour the hot vinegar over them until it overflows when the lid is closed.

> *This is best kept for several weeks before using. Check after one then two weeks to see whether the vinegar level needs to be topped up – you can just add plain distilled malt vinegar.*

> *This adds a spicy zing to a meat dish flavour and is very tasty. I have reduced Lady Ann's amounts of ginger and garlic considerably, in line with later recipes. If you are partial to hot curries and would like a strong flavour, the garlic and maybe ginger could be increased, even doubled, to your taste. The vegetables used can be varied according to what is available, and it is certainly worth trying asparagus.*

CB&O

To make Spanish Custard.

Take a pint of Cream, three spoonfulls of rice flower, the whites of 3 eggs well beaten, & four spoonfulls of fine sugar. Stir these well into your Cream cold; then take a few blaunached Almonds & beat them in a Morter with 2 spoonfulls of water, then Strain them into your Cream, & boyl it till it comes from the Skillet. Then take it up & put in 2 spoonfulls of sack, & wet your Cups with Sack, & put in your Custard, & let it stand till it is Cold. You may Stick sweetmeats on it if you please.

Ingredients:

1 tablespoon ground almonds
1 tablespoon orange-flower water
2 small eggs
1 level tablespoon golden caster sugar
¾ oz (20 g) rice flour
8 fl oz (240 ml) extra thick cream
2 tablespoons sherry

Stir the orange-flower water into the ground almonds and leave to stand while preparing the next stage or, for a stronger flavour, beat blanched almonds with the orange-flower water as in the original recipe. Beat the egg whites until frothy and add these, the sugar and the rice flour to the cream. Push the almonds through a strainer into the cream mix. Pour all into a thick-bottomed pan and stir over a low-moderate heat until the custard thickens and leaves the sides. (Approx. 15 minutes.) Remove from the heat and stir in one table-spoon of sherry. Pour another spoonful of sherry from one dish to another, wetting the sides before serving the custard into them. Serve when cold decorated with small pieces of wafer biscuit, gingerbread (see page 10), or the apricot chips on page 17.

This is a delicious, quick and easy sweet with a smooth texture and gentle flavour.

To Bake a Pike. (Mrs. Chauncy)

Take for a Pike of about 4 pound, half a lb. of suet finely shred, the Liver of the fish, some grated bread, a very little time, & nutmeg, some pepper & salt. Work it together with the yolk of an Egg and put it in the belly of the fish, & sow it up. An hour & half will bake it. You must do the fish over with an egg & put some Crumbs of bread & peices of butter, to keep the dish from melting when it comes out of the oven. Pour away the butter and send it up with strong Gravy sauce.

Pike is no longer a usual fish for the table.

CB80

To make Bombard Apples.

Take large apples, pare them & scope out the Core, & fill them with preserved apricots & some with Orange. Have some Puff paste role'd out very thin & put it round them like Dumplings; bake them in a gentle oven in a dish. Take the whites of eggs very well beat, a spoonfull of orange flower water put to it, double

90

refine'd sugar beat & sifted, & a little starch, & beat it a pretty while & ice the apples all over with it while they are hot, & set them in a warm place. They make a very pretty side dish; they are not to be used till quite cold, & the iceing quite cold.

Ingredients:

12 oz (340 g) puff pastry
4 large apples
Preserved apricots (see recipe on page 20)
2 egg whites
1 teaspoon orange-flower water
1 teaspoon cornstarch
3 oz (85 g) golden caster sugar

Roll the puff pastry out thinly in circles large enough to fold round the whole apples. Wash and core the apples. Fill the centres with the preserved apricots and a little of the jelly with them. Score lines towards the centre of the pastry so that it will fold around the apple leaving some pastry in the folds to allow for spreading as it cooks (see the illustration). Brush the pastry with a little milk and bake in a deep dish at 180°C for about 45 minutes, until the pastry is cooked. 'Icing' is optional due to the risk of Salmonella.

Beat the egg whites well, add the orange-flower water and beat again. Sprinkle over the sugar, then the cornflour and mix again until you have a thick white coating to apply to the hot baked apples. Set them in a top oven if you have used the lower one to cook them, or in a really warm place. When the 'icing' has set move the apples to a cool place and when cold into the refrigerator.

Brandy Cake. (Mrs. Morice's)

Take four pounds of flouer well dryed & sifted, seven pounds of curants washed & rubed clean, 6 pounds of butter, two pounds of almonds blanched & beat fine with orange flower water & sack. Then take 4 pounds of eggs, put away half the whites, 3 pounds of good Lump sugar pound'd & sifted, mace & nutmegs to your taste, half a pint of Brandy & half a pint of sack & what sweetmeats you like.

How to mixt the cake :-

Work ye Butter to a cream with your hands, then put in your sugar & almonds: mix these all well together & put in your eggs. Beat them till they Look thick & white, then put in your Sack & Brandy, & shake in your flouer by degrees & when your oven is ready, put in your Curants & sweatmeats, just before you put it in your hoop. It will take four hours in a quick oven to bake it.

Ingredients:

12 oz (340 g) butter
6 oz (170 g) golden caster sugar
4 oz (120 g) ground almonds
1 dessertspoon orange-flower water
4 egg yolks + 2 egg whites
2½ fl oz (75 ml) sherry **or** brandy
8 oz (225 g) 81% wholemeal SR flour
¾ teaspoon nutmeg (or to taste)
¼ teaspoon mace (or to taste)

14 oz (400 g) currants
Apricot chips (optional)

Cream the butter and sugar and then stir in the ground almonds and orange-flower water. Beat or blend the eggs until thick and pour in, mixing well. Add the sherry or brandy, and then sieve the flour, nutmeg and mace in a little at a time. Stir in the currants and chopped apricot chips and spoon into a round or square cake tin. Bake at 170°C in a fan-assisted oven for approximately 2 hours, turning the heat down to 150°C after 1 hour.

A beautiful, moist cake for special occasions. Lady Ann would have beaten the almonds with orange-flower water and sack to add moisture and flavour. With ready-ground almonds, the orange-flower water can simply be added to the mix. Sherry is substituted for the sack at the end of the recipe; it is not necessary with the almonds.

CR&D

Apricock Marmelade.

A pound of Sugar to a pound of apricocks before they are Stoned. Half a pint of Codlin or white currant liquor, which must be boyled very well with ye sugar, & scum'd. Then cut the apricocks into the Syrrup as fast as possible: wipe them clean but don't pare them. It must boyl till it flakes from the spoon: put in the kernels two or three minutes before you take it off the fire.

Ingredients:

3 medium or 2 very large cooking apples,
1 lb (450 g) golden caster sugar
15 fl oz (440 ml) water
1 lb (450 g) fresh apricots

Wash and chop each apple into six pieces and place in a covered pan with the water. Boil until mushy. Put through a jelly bag and leave to drip.

Put ½ pint (300 ml) of the cooking apple liquor into a pan and dissolve the sugar into it over a low heat. Bring to the boil and boil fast for 10 minutes. Meanwhile, slice the apricots in half lengthways, remove the stones and slice each lengthways again into six pieces. Put them into the boiling liquor and bring the marmalade back to the boil. Boil for a further 30-35 minutes when the colour will darken. Pour into two jars.

Marmalade in Lady Ann's day was solid to ensure keeping. We do not need, and may not like, it to be as concentrated as hers. There is no need to boil it beyond a toffee consistency – at this stage it tastes rich and delicious and can still be spread. It will be a matter of experiment to find your personal preference. Adding one or two apricot kernels will give a strong almond flavouring: if you wish to do this, take the stones from the centre of 2 apricots, wrap them in a cloth and give them 2 or 3 sharp taps with a pestle or heavy rolling pin, or use nutcrackers to open them. Inside you will find a white kernel. Blanch this in scalding water to remove the skin and then add to the marmalade for the last few minutes of boiling. I prefer to remove them before pouring into the jars.

Trotter jelly : a Strengther.

Take four Trotters, Split them and put them into an
Earthen pot with two ounces of Hartshorn shavings,
one small Nutmeg grossly powder'd, a quart of new
milk, & three pints of Water. Tye down the pot close
with brown paper, and bake it with Household Bread.
Strain it while hot throu a Sieve- See that the pan is
very dry - When it is cold, scum off the fat clear, &
put it in a cool place, not damp. It will keep in hot
weather three or four days. You may add to the above
a quarter of a pound of Raisins stoned. Take a
quarter of a pint at a time, two or three times a day,
with Rose Water & fine Sugar to your taste.

> *I remember my mother cooking pigs trotters, but
> for our dog to enjoy rather than the family. This
> had a good reputation at the time.*

◌◌◌

To Whiten Cloth.

Take Sheep's dung, new made in May or June, or
any time of ye Summer; which putt into a soft
water, & stir it together till it is well broken & pretty
thick. Then power it into a sive plac'd over a tub, that
will easyly contain all ye Cloth; so that it may be all
over cover'd with this water. Lay ye cloth in this
green water on Satturday morning, letting it soake
in it till Munday morning; then lay it out upon ye
grass by a pond, or river side, which is better; keep it
there, constantly wetting with pond or river water;

95

lett it lye out munday, teusday, & Weadnesday, observing to turn it every day; on Weadnesday beat it out & lay it in pond water all night; ye next day lay it out & water it till ye afternoon. Then forbare, that it may have time to dry before night; then putt it dry into a tubb, being wash'd clean, laying a buck sheet over it. Upon ye Buck sheet putt good store of Greens – viz.. Mercury, Mallows, Kecks* or wormwood, all or any of these. Then have in readyness a strong lye, which pour boyling hott upon ye greens, that it may descend to ye cloth; then cover it, greens & all, close, that it may keep all night. On Friday morning lay it on ye grass again, & keep it with watering all morning, only so that it may be dry against night. Then take ye same lye & make it boyling hott, & pour it upon ye cloth with fresh greens as you did before. On Saturday Morning, lay it out & order it as on friday, yet lett it ly in ye lye close till munday morning. Then lay it out upon ye grass, every day watering it with pond water till it is white enough.

This unlikely recipe is the one that brought me together with the descendants of Lady Ann Blencowe.

০৪৪০

*wild angelica

Lady Ann Blencowe's Physical Receipts

In the cookery section many of Lady Anne's recipes may be suitably made and enjoyed today. With her medicinal recipes the situation is very different. Many contain dangerous ingredients and should NOT be experimented with. Mrs. Barnardiston's gargle, the emulsion for sick people and the garlic plaster for the feet stand out as simple and safe homely recipes. With enthusiasm and a well-stocked garden one of the surffet waters might also be made. I have certainly found it a striking recipe and possibly helpful after a few months when the initial fiery effect of the spices has calmed down.

It was usual at the end of the 17th century to include recipes for treating horses in such a book and we see Lady Ann takes interest in the well being of cattle too. The recipe to keep rust from iron and the weapon salve help us to appreciate the breadth of knowledge house-keeping required at this period.

The problems she expects to treat within her family and wider household include, not surprisingly, the every-day pains, bruises, burns, colds, sore mouths, over-eating and constipation liable to trouble healthy people from time to time. She also caters for more serious com-plaints. It appears someone in the household suffers from dropsy as we find three recipes included. The rec-ipe for asthma is an official one bearing a doctor's name and certainly not in the class of 'home remedy'. It is intriguing to think she may have made it, but it is more likely that she was given this prescription to take to an apothecary at a later date and noted it here.

There are several remedies for the nerves, suitable for hysteria, low spirits or convulsions and pleurisy water that could also be given for children's fits. These are not unusual in a household book. The diet drink for the spring was clearly administered to all to re-balance the digestion after winter foods and the richness of the cookery recipes earlier in the book may well have contributed to the number of recipes here for 'surffet'.

The recipes against plague, pox, measles, burning fever and against consumption and scrophula, are a potent reminder of the precarious times she lived in.

It is plain from the ingredients that although numerous herbs still appear, she is moving with the times and using 'chymical medicine'. The range of ingredients in her recipes is considerable and they are worth reading simply to explore the fascinating variety of gum resins, spices, mineral salts, metals, drugs, mineral earths and herbs from many parts of the world. These apparently included the very expensive antidotes and panaceas for everything from plague to old coughs, Theriac and Mithradatium.

To aid enjoyment of this section I have added explanatory notes, detailing actions of herbs in some of the recipes and explaining the nature of unfamiliar ingredients and some of their sources at the time, in others.

We may visualise Lady Anne in a fascinating, well-stocked stillroom, supervising making these recipes and wonder at her knowledge and experience.

Lady Gage's Receipt for a Dropsy.

Take one Large Spoonfull every night & morning of unbruised mustard seed, drinking after each spoonful ½ a pint of the following decoction.-Take 3 Large Handfulls of the Green top of Broom, boil them in one Gallon of water, keep Scumming of it; when there is no more scum take it off the fire & when cool pour it into an earthen vessel with the Broom. Of this decoction Lady Betty has continued taking ever since ye 23rd of June last, & will continue taking of it till Spring. Mustard seed is a great strengthener of the Bowells, & Broom a great Dieretick, so much as to fill a common chamber pot in 24 hours. The third days takeing the Medicine took away entirely her thirst; she is now neither swell'd in body nor Legs, no more then she was five years agoe. She is grown fatter & can walk an hour together without difficulty.

> Dropsy was a much more common condition at this time and the water retention could, as is related; be relieved with a strong diuretic such as Broom, (Cytisus scoparius). The dosage of broom needs to be correct as it contains toxic alkaloids and is a herb classified for professional use only. Anecdotes of poisoning can be found in various literature. The handful measurement leaves one hoping any person repeating this recipe knew exactly how much was meant.

ભૂટ

To make Surffet Water.

Take a quart of Aqua Vitae, two Handfulls of Popeys, ye blacks being taken away, two handfull of ye flowers of Gilleflowers, & two handfull of ye flower of Marigolds, half a pint of red rosewater, two Nutmegs sliced, ye like quantity of mace, & more of Cinamon, ye like qnty of Ginger, half a quarter of a pound of raisins of ye sun stoned. Putt all these into a wide mouth'd glass, & sett it in ye sun 9 days. Then strain it & put to it half a pound of sugar; so keep it for your use.

Ingredients:

15 red roses
½ pint (300 ml) water
1 handful red poppy (*Papaver rhoeas*) petals
1 handful pinks (*Dianthus caryophyllus*)
1 handful pot marigold (*Calendula officinalis*) petals
1 pint (600 ml) brandy
2 half nutmegs
2 teaspoons mace pounded
Half cinnamon stick flaked
2 pieces fresh ginger (¾ in or 2 mm long) each
1 oz (30 g) raisins
8 oz (225 g) golden caster sugar

To make red rose water, take 15 red roses and slice away the base of each to remove the white heels at the bottom of the petals, tip out the pollen and set the petals in a small pan. Pour over half a pint (300 ml) of water and cover tightly with a lid. Set the pan on a very low heat so that the water just simmers gently with the occasional bubble rising – you should not hear it bubbling. Try not to keep looking or you will let out the essential oil with the steam. Leave it on the heat for 20 minutes and then set aside with the lid left closed for 2 hours. You will now find the colour of the roses has gone into the water and the perfume is wonderful.

Meanwhile prepare the other flowers by removing stamens and, in the case of the pot marigolds, the centre and washing the petals in cold water then drying them on paper kitchen towel or a clean tea towel. Cut off the white heels of the pinks.

Pour the brandy into a glass jar and add the flower petals. Add two nutmegs from which you have already grated half away, 2 pieces of sliced fresh ginger root, cinnamon, mace and the raisins. When the red rose water is ready, strain and add ¼ pint (150ml) to the brandy mix.

Set the covered jar in the window for nine days, swirling lightly each day. Strain and add the sugar, stirring until it is dissolved. Bottle. Keep for six months to allow the heat of the spices to blend in, giving a smooth, delicious medicine. Take 1-2 teaspoons.

The brandy of this time (aqua vitae) *was stronger than ours and so I have added 20 fl oz rather than 16 fl oz, the pint of Lady Ann's day. If you do not have sufficient flower petals ready at the same time, the petals (roses excepted) can be picked and stored layered in sugar until you have sufficient to make the recipe. Remove the petals and add this sugar at the end in the normal way. Using nutmegs that are already started saves the problem of slicing them.*

101

This is a powerful, amazing remedy and, if you try it too soon, prepares you for fire-eating. However, ginger and cinnamon are well known to assist with digestive problems, the Calendula, rose water and red poppy petals would all be soothing and healing to the stomach. Gillyflowers (the old name for pinks and carnations) are not used in modern herbal medicine but were commonly taken at this time to counteract melancholy.

CR80

For a cold in ye head

Take sage leaves, rub them & apply them to ye nostrils in ye morning.

If the leaves were simply rubbed and applied exactly as stated it seems unlikely to help. If, however, they were bruised and boiling water added to make an inhalation this would have effect. It may be that this was intended but too obvious to write down.

CR80

Syrup of St. Johns wort:
good for consumption, coughs & cold that stuffes ye stomache; or for inward bruises.

Take a gallon of spring watter, then take St. Johns wort leaves, stalks & flowers & bruise it very well, & put it into ye water. Put in soe much as when put it doune with your hand, ye water may stand two intches above ye earbe; Let it stand 20 houers; then

straine it off & stamp & bruis fresh earbs, as before, &
let it stand 10 houers. Then straine it offe againe,
put in fresh as before & let it stand 10 houers; & then
strain it off & to every pint of ye liquor put a pound
of sugar, or soe much as will make it a good syrup.
In a consumption or cold take 3 spoonfull of it in a
morning fasting & 2 or 3 spoonfull at a night.
Sometimes take it by it selfe & somtimes in a little
warme beare: thay with consumption doe well to
drink noe other drinke but what has St. Johns boiled
in it; instead of hops somtime add a handfull of firr
shaving to boile with ye St. Johns wort, to every
gallon of wort one handfull of St. John wort.
Somtimes boile firr shavings & St. John wort in
water & sweeten it with ye syrup to Drinke of
sometimes between meals for variety in
consumptions.

St. John's wort (Hypericum perforatum) is not
generally associated with treating chest problems
today, although it has antibacterial and antiviral
properties and aids the immune system. This application is seen traditionally however and is interesting and possibly effective. The fresh, green tips of
fir trees were commonly used to make ales and
drinks. We find John Pechey (1694) refers in his
herbal to the fir tree, (Picea abies) and describes
these trees as planted in gardens. He writes, "The
branches and Tops are infus'd in Diet-drinks for the
Scurvy, with very good Success". Picea abies is the
Norway spruce known to us more familiarly as the
Christmas tree. The new young shoots would be

tastier in this application and might well have added Vitamin C. The young trees were also the source of medicinal Venice Turpentine, an ingredient we will meet in a later recipe.

⊂ℨ℧

To strengthen ye eyes

Let another that is young chow annyseeds & then breath upon ye partys eyes.

This whimsical recipe would need to be magical to work and has the ring of an old superstition or spell. It is the only one like it and may have been included from an older recipe collection because it intrigued Lady Ann.

⊂ℨ℧

For the Green Sickness

Take 2 ounces of filed steele; putt itt in a melting pan, & lett it be red hott. Then punn it small, & seirce it through a Tiffany, mix with it one ounce of Cinamon beaten to very fine powder. Then take ½ a pound of loaff sugar, wett with so much water as is convenient to boyl almost to a candie hight, then putt in ye steelet Cinamon. Then stirr it and pour it out into a pewter Bason; & if it be cold, then cutt it into peices, & weigh it into parts, a pennyweight to be eaten att a time, in a morning fasting fast 3 hours after it. Fast 3 hours after dinner & then take it again, & fast 3 hours after it. Every day take of ye pills call'd ye Raffie pills, half an hour before dinner. Take so much as will give 2 or 3 stooles a day. Ye patient must eat fruit, nor salt meat, nor milk meats.

This is a condition commonly referred to in household recipe books, from additional explanation elsewhere it may refer to anything from stomach pain, perhaps accompanied by a greenish pallor on the face of the sufferer, to bilious vomiting, travel sickness and possibly jaundice.

Purgatives are a common element in widely varying cures for this condition. Here the filed steel would need to be beaten until it was very fine and was given to purge the system. It seems strange to us that anyone would take such a thing but the Pharmacopoeia's of the day contained many such ideas. The 'scientific' theory of the time supported this treatment because the specific weight and solidity of the metal were seen as correct for it to be taken up by the blood. Once in the bloodstream the sharp particles of both iron and steel were credited with cutting through obstructions, making this an 'opening' medicine. The sugar, Quincy tells us helps in the great labour of making the steel fine enough. It would also make the preparation easier to take. Perhaps this is why Lady Ann adds over four times the amount of sugar included in the recipe as prepared in hospitals. The cinnamon was included to protect the digestion from the results, by easing colic.

CB80

A drink for ye Green Sickness

Take Mugwort, penny Royall, Roman wormwood of each a good handfull, boyl them in 2 gallons of small Ale wort instead of Hopps & when it's boyld, strain it, work it with Barm, & when its turn'd, then putt in a pint of ye juice of scurvygrass & half a pound of horse reddish sliced & half a pound of ye filing of Rusty old iron. Lett it stand 10 days & drink a glass in a Morning, & att 4 a clock in ye afternoon. Use exercise.

This is actually a medicinal ale. The herbs included are all purgative to varying extents and the Artemisias, (Mugwort – A. vulgaris and Roman wormwood – A. absinthium) would possibly expel worms and certainly stimulate the liver. The juice of Scurvygrass (Cochlearia officinalis), was normally given along with aniseeds or cinnamon to ease the purgative effect. Here, pennyroyal (Mentha pulegium) has been added in this role. The horseradish was looked upon as strengthening the stomach and digestion, while acting as a stimulating diuretic to clear obstructions.

The considerable addition of iron was not being given to the patient in the role we see patients given iron supplements today. The sharp particles of iron qualified it for the same role as the steel in the recipe above. Although it was noted that iron caused constipation, in his English Dispensatory Quincy (1736), explains that while particles of iron were being forced along in the blood they didn't touch the sides and so did not cause coagulation. Instead, pushing through any obstructions, the iron thinned the blood and produced thinner body fluids, including an increase in urine. He does, alarmingly point out that where veins are contorted the blood vessels may break as the iron passes through.

CXEO

Mrs. Bennett's receipt for Sinews Shrunk

Stone horse* fatt rendred, putt in a litle savin into it, & boyl them together, & anoint ye sinews every day for a good while together, warm'd, & it will extend them.

The savin, Juniperus sabina, is more powerful in having a different essential oil content to Juniperus communis, a herb used today in herbal medicine. Savin can be very irritant, even applied externally. Clearly when Lady Ann made these recipes she was aware through what she had been taught and her own personal experience of exactly how much 'a little' savin meant. The quantity of solid horse fat is also left to the reader to determine.

CXEO

The Weapon Salve.

Putt a piece of Rusty Bacon, & heat ye tongs redd hott in ye fire & putt ye bakon between, & lett it drayn. into a Gally pott, & keep it for your use, anointing ye weapon with it & sett it dry.

---

*A gelding

CRED

To make a drink for ye spleen:
to be taken after vomiting or without, for ye clearing ye blood & for ye spleen pain in ye head or side.

Take ye roots of osmond-Royall, succory, fennill, parsly, polypody of ye oake, cleansed & very small, then bruised - of each one ounce & halve; bark of ye root of capers grosly powdered, halfe an ounce; rosmery flowers, a dram and halfe; of Zedory grosly powdered, a dram and halfe; powder of cream of tartar, halfe an ounce; filings of Steelle, or ye flakes that flie of from ye Smith's Anvill, 2 or 3 ounces, tied by itself in a thin linnin bag large. So hang it by a sling in a pipkin that it may not touch ye bottom or side. Put in of ye best sena one ounce, 3 quarts of spring water; boyl all this in a pipkin so clos'd down with a paste that no steem can gett out for 2 hours. Then lett it stand till it be cold before it be opened & strain'd. Then in part of ye Liquor dissolve 2 ounces of Mana over ye fire & strain it. So mingle it all together to be boyld & well cork'd for use.

Of this drink, a quarter of a pint every morning. It will give 2 or 3 stools in ye afternoon. This doe for sometime together. Fresh must be made before ye other be quite out.

A number of these ingredients will not be familiar to modern readers. Osmond-Royall (Osmunda regalis) was also known as water fern, Gerard remarks on it growing in a bog on Hampstead Heath. The heart of the root was included in 'wound drinks' to clear the blood of clots. The role of the spleen in medical thought of this time was to attract and store excess black bile. Dissection had shown the black matter to be there, resembling blood cells seen when blood separates out and so this clearing quality made it an herb of choice for the spleen.

Succory is wild chicory, (Cichorium intybus) considered a cooling and bitter herb suited to treating obstructions, particularly of the liver. Fennel and parsley are more familiar diuretic and flavouring herbs. Polypody of the Oak is actually a kind of fern growing on the oak tree. Gerard lists it as Polypodium quercinum *and advises that the boiled root removes 'cholericke' humours. Capers were also looked upon as a specific remedy for the spleen.*

Zedoary, (Curcuma zedoaria) is related to turmeric. The dried rhizome was listed as hot and dry by Pechey, good for looseness, vomiting and windy colic. Although it is an Indian herb and requires heat and protection in this climate I have found it a fascinating plant to grow came. The rounded rhizome is yellow when cut open and has a slightly camphoraceous/ ginger smell.

The steel is explained on page 105 and Senna (Cassia

senna) *came from India. The most intriguing ingredient here is Mana. Pechey writes about it in some detail as his friend and advisor, the great botanist, John Ray had seen Mana gathered while travelling in Italy. There seems to have been some controversy as to whether it was dew from the ash tree, an idea favoured by Culpeper. Pechey is certain of his information however as he writes,* "as has been prov'd by undoubted experiment" *that Manna is the juice distilling from the trunk or branches of the ash tree. This juice, he wrote, sweated out and hardened in the sun. The best, he informs us came from Calabria.*

CRED

To Make the Redball

Take Cardas, tormentell, bettany, pimpernell, angelicoe, dragon Baum, violet leves, Strawbery Leves, Rosmery, dandelion, sage, peletary, Burage, suckery, St. Johns wort, egremone, ribwort; of each sort a handfull. Chop them very small & steep them in a gallon of white wine 24 hours. Take 2 pounds of ye powder of Bolarmenack; wett it as Morter with this Liquar well straned. Put in fresh herbs every day into the wine for 3 days. Then mix it & sett it in ye sun in a bason & as it dries put in ye wine till it be all in, sturing it offten; keep it frome ye rain.

The large number of herbs contained in this recipe was not unusual. It contains herbs to aid the digestion such as sage (Salvia officinalis), *rosemary* (Rosmarinus officinalis) *and angelica* (Angelica archangelica).

Bitters to stimulate the digestive juices and work on the liver and bowel axis; dandelion root, (Taraxacum officinale*),* succory *(*Cichorium intybus*),* agrimony *(*Agrimonia eupatoria*) and milk thistle (*Carduus marianus*). There is also the astringency of tormentil root (*Potentilla erecta*) and the soothing, demulcent action of ribwort plantain (*Plantago lanceolata*).*

Pellitory of the wall (Parietaria diffusa*), is included for the kidneys and St. John's wort* (Hypericum perforatum*) was looked upon as an excellent diuretic at the time.*

The tiny, pretty scarlet pimpernel, (Anagallis arvensis*) was used for griping pains in children and so would be another calming digestive, while borage (*Borago officinalis*) cleared away melancholy. The leaves of* Viola odorata *were considered soothing and those of the wild strawberry (*Fragaria vesca*) astringent; both included for the comfort of the bowels. Dragon baum may refer to* Arum draconitum *used dried as a protector against poison. These together are tonic to the digestive and urinary systems. Bolarmenack is a natural earth, mainly imported from Armenia. The use of different earths in medicine was widespread and these were sold as blocks bearing the stamp of their origin as a mark of authentication. The greatest collection of samples of the many kinds can be seen in the Museum of Pharmacy in Basle. It is well worth a visit. Many of Lady Ann's unusual ingredients are on display there.*

Bolus armena *was Bolarmenack was properly known, may have contained some iron and produced an astringent effect. It was prescribed for diarrhoea and haem-*

orrhages. Quincy complained of it being much adulterated.

CR&&D

Drugs for ye red ball

Put in 6 peneworth of saffron; steep it in sack & strane it in an ounce of Venes treakle, an ounce of Methredate, 2 ounces of Diascordiam, half an ounce of alkermice, red Corall & pearl of each 2 drams, 2 books of leaf gold & stur them well together & let it dry. Then make in Balls & gild them.

Give to Man as Much as will Lay on a 6 pence; to a child, a 3 pence. If it be in a feaver, give a draught of Virginny snakeweed poset drink with it last at night or Sage poset drink; or if for ye small pox you may give it in sack.

This is quite an extravagant recipe, full of precious and expensive ingredients. When using saffron it is necessary to steep it in a liquid, the sack mentioned here would be rather like a sherry. Venus treacle, otherwise known as Theriaca Andromachi, (Andromachi was physician to the Emperor Nero) was made in Venice, hence the common name. There are far too many ingredients to be listed here. Suffice it to say that vipers were an essential part, together with opium, roots such as zedoary and liquorice, gums, including myrrh and frankincense, spices, saffron and many other herbs and seeds. A great many fraudulent concoctions were sold as Venice treacle for less than the exorbitant price of the real thing. A London treacle was also made, the

112

recipe appears in Culpeper's English Physician En-larged. One wonders where Lady Ann obtained hers and whether it was the real thing.

Mithradate was a similarly important polypharmic antidote and panacea made with much ceremony and named after Mithridates VI Eupator, King of Pontus in the first century B.C. He was an expert on antidotes to poisons. The recipe appears to have survived in use over the 1,700 years from his time to Lady Ann's.

Diascordium was yet another polypharmic mixture of spices, gums, opium, astringent roots, Armenian bole and pepper. The powders were mixed to an electuary, or soft paste with clarified honey and sugar of roses. Quincy notes it being used by mischievous nurses to make children sleep.

He also writes that the juice of the berries of Ilex acule-ate, *listed here as alkermice (Alkermes) is a fine cordial.*

Red coral had a reputation for being effective against children's convulsions. Many claims were made for the cures from the absorbent qualities of pearls and leaf gold was still a fashionable inclusion. Quincy pointed out however that gold is not digestible in the stomach and therefore it was simply added according to earlier erroneous beliefs and to raise the price of the medicine.

The Virginian snakeweed for fever refers to (Aristolochia serpentaria) *imported from America as an aromatic fever medicine.*

CRSO

To pull off hair

Two ounces of wax & one ounce of rosen & boyle it a great while togeather till you see it stif, which you may try by dropping it on a spoon. Wash ye place with juce of temitry to keep ye hair from comeing again.

An isolated cosmetic recipe for the brave!

෨෫ဃ

Emullion for Sick people

Take barley water, and to a pint of that take 12 Almonds blanch'd & beaten & strained into it; but for an Asma, putt liquorish, great dayzys in ye water, first boyle with ye Almons.

This emulsion is at last a harmless, homely recipe. Liquorice is indeed good for asthma. Presuming the 'great dayzys' to be Ox-eye (Chrysanthemum leucanthemum), they too were formerly included in tonic drinks.

෨෫ဃ

To Make a Cordiall Water:

good against any Infections, as ye Plague, Poxe, Measles, burning feaver, & to remove any offensive or Venomouse Matter from ye Hart or Stomach, or to be used after surfetts or in Passion of ye Mother, or for Children in fitts or Convulsions, & is generally good to comfort or strengthen Nature.

Take of Sage, .Salandine, Rosemary, wormwood, Rosa Solis, Mugwort, Pimpernell, Dragons, Scabious, Egrimony, Balme Scordium, Carduus, Bettony flowers & leaves, of Each a good handfull. Then take ye Roots of Tormentile, Angelica, Ellencampane, Piony, Zeduary, Liquorish, of all cleane scrap'd ½ an Ounce. Lett all ye Herbs be wash'd & shak'd in clean linen cloath, untill they be very dry. Then shred them all togeather, & lett ye Roots he shred thinn, & mix'd with ye herbs. Then put them all to a gallon of white wine, & lett them steep togeather an a large Gally Pott or earthen One well glas'd; and so lett them remaine close cover'd 2 days & 2 nights stiring them once every day. Then distill them in an Ordinary still, not in a limbeak*, with a soft fire, reserving about a pint of ye First runing in a glass by itself for ye strongest, as also a quart of

*Alembic: an early type of retort still

115

ye Second runing by itself, and lastly about a pint of ye last & weakest sort by itself, in severall glasses close stopt with cork & fast bound with leather, for Your use.

Note also that it is good to close ye Still round with paste made of Rye meale, Vinegar, Whites of Eggs & Bole almoniack. Of ye first sort of this Water may be given to any Man or Woman, though she be with Child, one or two spoonsfull. Of ye third & weakest sort, you may give to Young Children a spoonfull safely. This Water to Comfort is usually· given luckwarm with a little sugar or Sugar Candy, & may be given also cold; and is most properly given when ye Stomack is empty. And also it may very fittly be mix'd with any Julip where there is any infection fear'd. But neither this nor any other hott waters should be used ordinaryly, but where ye party hath need of such helps.

What a wonderful sight it must have been with all the herbs and roots laid ready for this recipe! It was perfectly usual for waters intended to treat the Plague and/or Pox to have this many ingredients or more. We can only guess at the combined effect. There are certainly a number of antibacterial, cleansing and anti-inflammatory herbs amongst them. The careful instructions for distilling and dispensing the water show this to be a valued recipe actually made by Lady Ann.

CRWO

For Dropsy
(Coz. Botry's* receipt from London)

Take the Ashes of Burnt juniper two good handfuls;
the ashes of Burnt Broome as much; Juniper berries,
4 Ounces; beaten Dran of Elder, 2 Handfulls; a
Sprig of Wormwood, one pound of Raisins of the
Sun Ston'd. Put them all into a thin Linnen bag
with a pibble in to, into a Barrel of smal Ale of three
or four gallons. After it has done spurging, let it
stand three days & then drink of it, and drink of no
other Beer but this. When it is gone make more untill
you are well. - Be sure not to putt the things into the
Drink untill it has done Working.

*This is a recipe for interest only and not to be tried at
home!*

C3&O

Aqua Mirabilis.

Take of ye juice of mint, Balme, Burridge,
salandine, of each one pint; Cububs, Gallingals,
Curdimuny, mollilot flowers, of each two Drams;
ginger & nutmeg of each half an ounce; mace,
cinamon, of each one dramm; aniss & fennil seeds,
if you like them, of each half an ounce. Beat them all
grosly; put them into an earthen vessel with ye juces.
Then add to them 3 quartes of sack or any spirits,

*Sir John's sister Joyce married John Botry (Buttery) of Marston St
Lawrence in 1670

one quart of brandy, one pint of Angellico water, one pint of red rose-water. Cover them close & let them stand 44 hours; then distill them. You may add what cordial flowers are to be gotten.

Either Lady Ann, or her source for this recipe has added the juices of mint, lemon balm and borage and the melilot flowers to the Dispensatory prescription with this name. The juices would soften the flavour and soothe the effects of the powerful greater celandine (Chelidonium majus), which has a restricted dosage today.

Melilotus officinalis appears also in similar 18th Century household recipes despite Pechey listing them as not commonly given internally. Cubebs, galingale, cardamom, ginger, nutmeg, mace and cinnamon add a good deal of digestive spice. Anise was regarded at the time as a hot seed and may be added here with fennel to combat any griping. Both angelica and red rose-waters could have been made in her stillroom and would be comforting to the stomach.

CR80

To cause one to make watter when stoped

Take 3 leaved grass brused & heated between two tiles & apply hot to ye share bone: causeth you to make watter.

Three-leaved grass could refer to any one of several clovers. The only one given by Gerard as having a diuretic effect however, is treacle clover, (Trifolium bituminosum).

118

Past to wash hands

Blanch a pound of Almons, bitter ones, & pound them in a stone morter, & in the pounding put in half of Ox gals be degrees as you pound them. Then bake the yolks of 6 egges, beat very well in a poringer with littel of the ox gals. Then put it into the Morter to ye almons. Then put in half a pint of sack & 3 peney worth of Oyl of Tarter; work it well to gether. Then stone a pound of reasons of the sun and pound them in the Morter, taking out the other thing, & when they are very well pounded, put in the other things & incorprate it well together. Put it in a pot & cover it Cloas & set it in a cool place & it will keep 6 Mounths.

What an amazing collection of ingredients this is! I cannot see anyone using it today. Clearly the sack provided the alcohol to make it keep.

ೞ൏

To make ye teeth white

Take of burnt Date Stones & Corrall prepared, of each two dramms, mixed together into a whit linnen Cloth, & when it is steeped in wine rubb your teeth with it. It will make them whit & strong.

Although scouring the teeth, this powder might be rather harsh for their long survival!

ೞ൏

119

An Excellent Cearcloth for pains, bruises & burns

Take of oyl of olives, five pints, Red Lead two pound, white lead four ounces Camphir one ounce. Mix the leads with the Oyle by deagrees, & let it stand over a gentle fire, stiring it all ye while, till it be incorporate & of a darkish colour; after which, put in the camphir, beating it first with a litle Oyle. Keep it still stiring. After some time take out a spoonfull to cool that you may see when it is stiff enough to make up in Rolls. Do it over a chaifing dish of coals, for a flaming fire as very, dangerous least it shuld boil over & ye salve will not be so if it is done too quick: it should be 4 or 5 hours about.

At this time the use of red or white lead on the skin was usual. Red lead was prepared by melting lead and reducing it to a powder. White lead had been corroded by steeping it in vinegar. Quincy defines the consistency of a cerecloth being between those of an unguent (ointment) and a plaster. The recipe tells us that Lady Ann mixed the ingredients together over the heat until the mix was stiff enough to make into rolls to be kept for use.

CB80

For a Horse under a great cold or surfit
(Mr. Ledgand)

Boyl one third of a pound of aniseeds in a quart of Ale. Pour it on half a pound of honey in a bowl; brew or stir it about, till it is cool enough to gave in a horn to your horse. Keep him cloathed in the stable, & give him warm water night and morning: repeat this Cordial three days together, & take care he dose not catch cold.

It is usual to take about a quart of blood away before you begin with the cordial.

I am not qualified to comment on this recipe other than to note that the ingredients appear to be agreeable. Both honey and aniseeds are included in remedies for horses in Juliette de Bairacli Levy's Herbal Handbook for Farm and Stable. *She does not use ale but I well remember a horse stopping regularly with its rider outside a public house in Kent and both being served with beer. The horse certainly enjoyed this weekly tipple.*

CR&O

Surfeit Water

Two Gallons of Anniseed Water, half a bushell of Poppeys, & steep them in ye Anniseed Water for a fortnight. Cover them & stir them every Day. Then strain of ye poppeys & take 2 oz. of Anniseeds & 2 oz of Cardimum seeds, two Oz of Coriander seeds, 2 Oz of Liquorish sliced. Bruise ye seeds, figgs & Raisons, of each a pound. Ye Raisons being ston'd, put all these into ye Anniseed Water. After it have lain 3 or 4 Days strain it & bottle it off.

The poppies are red corn poppies (Papaver rhoeas). Distilling is no longer a household occupation.

C3EO

For a Horses cold (Mr. Blencowe)

Three ounces of rusty bacon, two Ounces of tarr, one ounce and half of good honey, half an ounce of flower of brimstone, worked up into a stiff paste with wheat flower. A ball or two given the Horse three successive mornings, and rest him two or three days. If need be, repeat them again.

It would be interesting to know which Mr. Blencowe provided this recipe.

C3EO

High Spirrited Pills

Salt of Steel 3 drams
Galbmam strain'd
Castor (the finest sort)
of each two drams.
Assafeetida
Salt of Amber of Each two Scruples.
Camphire

Make all these into little pills & take 3 at Night & 3 at Morn, with a little bitters after them.

This is a similar recipe to one in Quincy's Dispensatory. The uses of steel have been explained on page 105. Galbanum is a yellow resin that comes from the lower stem and roots of Ferrula gummosa. This is a tall, perennial umbelliferous plant native to central Asia. It is related to the asafoetida, also a Ferrula. This root was given in pills to stop fits of hysterics. The smell of it is so strong it has been nicknamed 'devil's dung'. Further pungent smells would be added by the presence of camphor and castor. Castor is castoreum, a substance produced by the glands of the male and female beaver. It is red and was popularly used in medicine for the nerves.

Salt of amber was considered to be active in cleansing the whole nervous system, the word 'scour'd' is used by Quincy. In fevers and nervous conditions this substance might be used to cut through secretions and clean the deepest recesses in the head. All matter removed was considered to be eliminated with the urine.

Three scruples equal one drachm therefore more than twice the quantity of the first three ingredients would be used to the rest.

CBEO

For ye stone

Take unsett Leeks, parsley roots, Bettany & Ivy Berrys. Braiz them all together, & temper them with white wine, & drink it first & last & it will break ye stone. In proof, lay a flint stone in ye medicine & it will break in 24 hours.

The parsley referred to will be parsley piert (Aphanes arvensis), *also known as parsley break-stone. Culpeper writes,* "its operation is very prevalent to provoke urine and to break the stone"....*In wine* "it would bring away gravel from the kidneys insensibly, and without pain". *Gerard mentions berries of ivy* (Hedera helix), *being given against the stone, although he does not recommend it. He thought them nauseating and unhelpful. The betony,* (Stachys betonica) *is also surprising in this context. The test to prove the power of the medicine sounds quite alarming. Not a recipe to try at home.*

CBEO

The Blessed Pills

Aloes, half an Ounce.

Assafet, Gallanua, Myrrh, of each one dram.

Gal Martis, six Drams.

Saffron, Mace, of each half a dram.

Oyl of Amber, 40 drops.

Of senna, two drams.

Syrrup of Mugwort, a sufficient quantity to make it into pills.

This recipe is filled with bitter resins and purgatives such as the aloes and senna. The oil of amber Quincy tells us was sometimes prescribed in nervous cases. The syrup of mugwort (Artemisia vulgaris) would also act as a bitter. The pills must have been strongly cleansing.

CB80

Mrs. Joynes Reseit for a Plaister for Corns

Take two ounces of Venice Turpintine and one ounce of virgin wax. Melt them togather and let it boyl a little. Then put it into a gally pott for your use. Spred it on a thick peace of Holland or Dowlace & put a plaister of it a little biger then ye Corne on your bottom of your foot or any other Part Agreaifed: keep it on as long as it will stick & the corne will beare peeling or Cutting of with care. If you Constantly ware it on the bottom of your foot, it will by degreas Cure ye corne.

Venice turpentine was obtained by boring into the larch tree Terebintha laricina, *grown in Switzerland and parts of France. The turpentine resin was exported from Venice, hence the name.*

CS80

Dr. Lower's Drops for Hysterick or Convulsion Fits:
approved for lowness of Spirits or Gidiness in the Head

Take a pint of the best Brandy and put into it one Ounce of Assafetida Bruised, with two spoon full of Wood Soot. Set this in a Bottle for Nine or ten Days and nights near a fire, shaking the Bottle twice or thrice a day: then let it stand, and when 'tis settled pour it off clear into a small Bottle, but keep it standing on the ground without moveing it, and whenever you are to use it pour it off the Clear.

For lowness of Spirits take 15, 20 or 30 Drops either in white wine or Black Cherry water, twice a day, and increase the dose till you come to a Teaspoonfull. 'Tis most admirable to strenghen the Nerves.

For fits of any sort, approved; give to a young Child from 8 to 12 drops in Black Cherry water; a bigger Child from 12 to 30 drops; and a grown person to a Tea spoonfull or two. It must be given twice a day, or an hour before the fit's expected, and three days before or three days after the change of the

126

Moon. 'Tis very good for wind in young children, tho' they have not fits, but in fits it does great cures, both in Grown. people and Children.

This was the main application for asafoetida at the time and I can only think it must have worked well or I cannot imagine anyone taking such a pungent medicine. The connection between children's fits and the moon may not be as close to witchcraft as might be imagined. Many studies have taken place on possible physiological effects on man by changing phases of the moon with certain effects being proven.

CB80

Mrs. Sherlock's Recept for a pain in ye head

2 ounces of Rubbarb, sliced, one ounce of Jensit's Bark in powder, 2 ounces of sugar Candy, 2 Drams of Juniper Berris, Sinamon and nutmeg of each a Dram; a Quart of wine infuse it in.

Cleansing of the system is once again the aim of the recipe with laxative rhubarb and diuretic juniper. Cinnamon and nutmeg are here to calm the gut. Juniper was also recommended at this time for diseases of the head and nerves. Jesuit's bark or cinchona was the favoured treatment for agues, but as Quincy warns, "there is a great deal of mischief to be done with it in ignorant Hands".

CB80

Plurecy Water

Likewise good for Grips & Fitts in Children

Take of Stone Horse Dung new made 8 pound, Anniseeds brused & licquorish sliced, of Each two Ounces, Raisins of the sun stoned 2 Ounces, & Venus Treacle one ounce. Put all these into 3 quarts of strong White wine; stir it well together & cover it & let it stand by the fire all night. The next Day still it in a Cold Still.

Without the horse dung this would be a more pleasant recipe. One hopes the stilling of it made it more palatable!

☙☙

For a Cough or Consumption.

(Miss Fountain)

Take 30 garden snails & 30 Earth worms of middling sise, bruise ye snails & wash them & ye worms in fair water, cut ye worms in peices. Boil these in a quart of Spring water to a pint. Pour it boiling hot on 2 ounces of Candied Eringo root sliced thin. When it is cold strain it thro' a flannel bag. Take a quarter of a pint of it warm, with an Equal quantity of Cows' Milk.

Continue this course till well.

This recipe looks as if it has come from the Middle Ages. However, we find garden snails used to treat consumption over a 200-year period. They were considered to be good for penetrating sticky mucus, perhaps because they produced something similar themselves, but I would be fascinated to know whether research might find an effective chemical constituent behind this popular cure. The worms were considered of a similar nature to snails but having more nitrous salt made them more penetrating in cleansing inflammations of the lungs. Candied eryngo root (Eryngium maritimum) was considered to be good for consumptive people as well as an enjoyable, aphrodisiac sweetmeat.

CB&O

A Plaister for a Cough (Lady Clarke)

Take Burgamy Pitch Rosin, & Bees wax, of each two ounces; melt them together; then take one ounce & half of oyle of mace. Melt all these together & spread it upon sheeps Leather, the fleshey side of the Leather.

Cut the Plaister like a heart & lay the broad side uppermost upon the Breast, pritty high, & cover over the Lungs & stomach. It must not be held by the fire but laid on & with the warmth of a hand on the one side; 'twill make it stick. When one plaister comes off Lay on another, & keep the stuff in a pot. This has done great cures.

Burgundy pitch resin came from Pinus abies and was included in the Pharmacopoeia of this time. It was probably sourced from Switzerland or Germany. Plasters can be very effective when applied to chest problems. The detail of this recipe is particularly interesting. Pechey recommends the mace as very penetrating in its heat.

Cঞৱৰৄৎৄ

For the King's Evil (Mrs. Dormar)

Burn spunge in a cruciple tell it is Red Hot, then sift it through a sive, & give as much as will lye on a shilling of the powder, in a morning and att four or five a clock in an evening, in two or three spoonfuls of Milk warmed; & while thay take it, let them Drink a pint or more, of Sanicle Tea in a day; & if they have sores, wash them with the Tea. You must not expect to find any effect, till you have continued this Medicine att least six weeks.

The King's evil, or scrophula most commonly affected the glands in the neck, with abscesses in the lymph nodes due to tuberculosis. Sponge was used to hold abscesses open to drain. Pechey records the practice of giving the ashes in wine for a bronchocele. This term could have been applied to a goitre. In a later Materia medica (1829) translated from the French it was recorded that a new discovery had vindicated the old practice of giving sponge in scrophula. It had been found that sponge contained small quantities of iodine that could be helpful. The sanicle tea would also be well suited to cleansing ulcerous conditions, both inwardly and outwardly.

Dr. Burbon's Prescription for a Sore throt
(Mr. Jackson*)

Take a Pint of milk & put into it one ounce of black pepper bruised. Let it boyl up twice or thrice on ye fire, then put it into a Pint China Bason. Take a Tundish whose top is of ye same wideness with ye top of ye bason, turning ye top downwards over ye top of ye bason & raping a Cloth Round it to keep in ye Steem, & force it all out at ye spout of ye Tundish. Put ye Spout in your mouth & let the Steam go down your throat for a quarter of an Hour.

I am not sure how comfortable this would be but perhaps the warming fumes would prove helpful.

⊂ॐ☾

To keep Iron from being touch'd with rust
(Mr. Jackson)

Melt & strain a pound of fresh Hogs Lard; put it into an earthen pipkin to dissolve gently over ye fire. When it is wholy dissolved put into that quantity half an ounce of Camphire finely powder'd & let it boyl till your Camphire be well dissolved in ye Liquor; then take it of ye fire, & while it is scalding hot, put into it as much black Lead finely powdered as will make ye liquor of a right lead colour. When

*Lady Ann's grand-daughter Jane married Rev Samuel Jackson (1709-1792) of Stisted in Essex. This would have been long after Anne's death but perhaps the contact between the families had been long-standing.

you use it let ye Iron be clean scoured & then with ye liquor scalding hot, let it lye on two dayes & then wipe it clean off again & they will not be subject to rust.

A really interesting recipe.

CSSO

Mr. Condre's receipt for Cattle after the bite of a Mad Dog

Wild mint, wild primrose roots, and English box: a little more of the box than the other things.

I imagine this would be a purgative cure. Herbals of this time agree that box is little used in medicine. Later, Sir John Hill's Family Herbal, *(1st edition 1754) gives the root as "an excellent medicine in all foulness of the blood". This suggests the root rather than the poisonous leaf of box was intended here.*

CSSO

A Receipt for Swell Legs, or jaundice

Break off the leaves of hartichoak plants as close to the great stem as you can. Take half a pint of the Juce of those leaves to a pint of Mountain Wine. Take a wine glass of it three times a day.

Artichokes were a very popular food. The medicinal effects of artichoke juice in cleansing the liver were very probably more appreciated by the housewife than now.

The Black Salve

Take a Pint of Eating Oyle of Red Lead 8 Ounces, Virgins Wax, 4 Ounces, Populeum 4 Ounces, Oyl of Roses one Ounce, Oyl of Cammomel one Ounse. Boyl all these together till they Look Black.

I have no knowledge of exactly what is meant by "eating oyle of Red lead", the nature of red lead was discussed on page 120. Oil of chamomile would be very soothing and with the oil of roses, counter some of the corrosive effect of the lead. Populeum may simply refer to the buds of the black poplar (Populus nigra). It most likely refers to Unguentum populeon, an ointment made from the buds.

෬෩

To make the Green Salve

Take of Sago Plantain, Mallows, of Each a Handful, 2 Pound of Mutton Suet. Chop them all well together & Boil Them in a brass Skillet over a Slow fire. Then Strain it into a Pot of cold water, let it Stand till next Morning. Then put it into the Skillet & Add to it a Pound of Bees Wax & 12 Ounces of Rosin, & 12 Ounces of Stone Pitch. Boyl them well together & - Strain it & keep it for Use.

I have searched without success for Sago Plantain and can only presume it to be Plantago major. *The mallows could equally well refer to marshmallow (Althaea officinalis), or the common mallow (Malva sylvestris). Either might be used in a salve with success. This*

133

would be a fairly stiff salve with a healing, soothing action from the herbs.

CʒᏠ

Dr. Meed's Certain Cure for the Bite of a Mad dog

Let the Patient be Blooded at the Arm, 9 or 10 Ounces. Take of the Herb Call'd in Latin Lichen *Cinercus Terrestris*, in English Ash Colour Liverwort, clean dried & Powder'd, half an Ounse, of black pepper two Drams. Mix these well together, & Divide the powder into 4 Doses, one of which must be taken every morning fasting, for 4 Mornings, Sussessively, in half a Pint of Cow's milk warm.

After these 4 Doses are taken, the Patient must go into the Cold Bath or Cold Spring or River every Morning fasting for a Month; he must be dipt all over, but not stay in with his Head above Water longer than half a Minute if the Water be very Cold; after this he must go in 3 times a week for a fortnight Longer.

N.B. the Lichen is a very Comon Herb, and grows generally in Sandy & Barren Soils all over England; the Right time to Gather it, is in the Months of October & November.

Lichen terrestris Cinereus, *or Ash-coloured Ground Liverwort is described by Joseph Miller in his Botanicum Officinale as a plant bearing neither flowers nor seeds, with thick crumpled, hollow leaves. He records it as a recent addition to medicine in 1722. This recipe must then have been very up to date.*

C3 80

Dr. Nintle's Receipt for an Asthma and Swell'd Legs

The Electuary. Take Rhubarb, Troches of Agaric in Powder, of each 4 Scruples. Myrrh, Gum Podellium, both Powder'd together, of Each one Dram. Red Roses, Shavings of Yellow Sanders, Root of Florentine Iris, Depurated Niter, of each in Powder 2 Scruples. Root of Turmerisk in Powder, 2 scruples. Cinamon, Spikenard, Saffron, Juniper Berries, in Powder, of each 1 Scruple. The Myrrh & the Gum Podellium shod be powder'd together, & the Bottom of the Mortar should be Rubbed first with 2 or 3 Drops of Oyl of Juniper, & then they should be mix't with all the other Powders in a Marble Mortar, & with three drams of Pulp of Squills Roasted in the Ashes, & one Ounce & Half of Conserve of Roman Wormwood, & one Dram of Venise Turpentine, first dissolv'd in a sufficient Quantity of Syrup of Horehound [to] be reduced into the Form of an Electuary.

The Dose of which Electuary is from one Dram & half to two Drams Every Morning fasting, & drinking after it the following Crawfish Broth. — Take half a Pound of Lean Veal Cut in Slices, The

135

Tails of Twelve live Crawfish with the Shell on them, Bruised in a Marble Mortar, three Ounces of the Root of Dandelion Bruised in a Marble Mortar. Put all this into an Earthen glazed Pan or Pipkin, with one Pint & half of Spring Water, & Let it boil very slowly over the Coals till the Liquor be Reduced to half, that is, Nine Ounses. About a Quarter of an Hour before it is taken from the fire, put in half a handful of Water Cresses Chopt, & cover the Pipkin; when it is done it shou'd be strained, & if not given immediately put into a Clean Pan & heated again when it is given.

The Patient should fast after it till dinner, and, when fair weather, Ride out in the Morning. Should not Drink above a Glass or two of Wine at Dinner. Should avoid drinking too much diluting Liquor, such as Tea. Should Sup lightly. It is apprehended that from this Electuary the Difficulty of Breathing & Swelling in the foot will be Sensibly releiv'd, that the Patient will be encouraged to Continue it some length of Time, it being no ways Inconvenient nor interfering with any Business whatever. Nay, that he will be encouraged to take it twice a day, that is the Quantity of a Small Nutmeg only at Supper time, drinking after it the Crawfish Broth as in the Morning & no other Supper.

It would seem likely this is a prescription to be taken to the apothecary. I can however imagine Lady Ann preparing some of these ingredients in her stillroom.

She would almost certainly have supervised gathering the rhizome of the Florentine iris in autumn and drying it to produce, one year later, a rich powder smelling of violets. This was used in medicine, cosmetics and scented mixtures. The last as a fixative. Yellow Sanders was a form of sandalwood imported from India, the others being white and red. In 1635 a levy of 2s per lb put on its importation made this an expensive ingredient. Troches of Agaric contained the fungus, white agaric and ginger. Gum Podellium may be presumed to refer to Bdellium gum, from a tree related to the Commiphora from which myrrh is obtained, Commiphora wightii. *Bdellium has been used to reduce inflammation. Spikenard probably refers to Celtic nard then known as Nardus celtica or Mountain French spikenard, a heating herb regarded as opening and good against "malignant distempers". (Miller 1722).*

CR80

For a swelling after a surfet, or for a Dropsy

After haveing taken several doses of Jollop, take musterd seed, horseredish, & filings of steele steeped in strong beer: to be taken 3 or 4 spoonfulls twice a day.

The Jollop was a purgative drug obtained from the tuberous roots of Ipomæa purga, *a Mexican climbing plant. The other ingredients are heating, stimulating to digestion and circulation, with the steel to cut through obstructions.*

CR80

A receipt to make ye Green Ointment that cured Lady Probyn's* Coachman's back
(Mrs. Lethiculear)

Take of Sage and Rue of each one handfull, of wormwood and bay leaves, each half a pound. Gather these in the heat of the Day. They must be unwashed and Shread small. And take a pound and half of sheep suet and stamp it with the herbs untill they be all of one couler; put it in a pint and half of the best Sallet Oil, and stir them well together, and put it in a pot and stop it close up, and let it stand nine days. Then boil it till the strength of the herbs be gon, and take care in boiling that, you doe not burn it. And when it is boil'd put in an ounce and half of Oil of spike, and keep it for your use. It is good for all manner of wounds, bruises, burns and sprains. The best time to make it is in May.

This is a typical early ointment for treating muscular aches and pains. Wormwood is no longer commonly used in external applications. Handling rue can produce a long-lasting blistering rash. I have previously made recipes with sage, bay and lavender

*The memorial tablet to Sir John Blencowe in the Church at Marston St Lawrence reads: '... *Married Ann eldest Daughter of the famous Dr Wallis. And had issue by Her Seven Children. Two died young. The others he saw married to his satisfaction. ...* ' One of these 'satisfactory' marriages was that of his second daughter Elizabeth to Sir Edmund Probyn who was Lord Chief Baron of his Majesty's Court of Exchequer.

and have found these very comforting and analgesic.
Oil of spike would be a rather powerful lavender oil.

☙❧

A power to cure a sore tongue or sore mouth : it cures a canker, will take away all lumps in the mouth or Gums, will fasten the teeth, and is good for the toothake

Take a quarter of an ounce of salt prunella, as much common salt as will lye on the top of a knife, rough allum the bigness of a nuttmegg, six drops of Vinegar. Put all these into the yolk of an Egg, having first pour 'd away the white. You must break the shell only a little at one end to let white run out; then put in your salts finely powder'd and drop in your Vinegar; then set your shell over wood embers; it will soon boyl. Stir it some times with a stick, keep it on the embers till it is so dry that no moisture is left in it. Be sure no coal come near it least it catch fire. If the shell burn on one side turn it on the other, till it is quite done, and when you find it is quite dry make a clear place on the hearth or put it, shell and all, into the middle of a clear fare. It will soon blaise & burn to a clear coal. When it has done blaising, take it out of the fire, and when cold pound it very fine. If the egg is small you may two yolks to this quantity of salt. — N.B. Your care must be not to let a Coal burn the shell before it is enough, least it catch fire. The manner of useing it is to wett your finger, dip it in the powder, and so apply it to the sore part. It will make it smart and draw a rhum. If you swallow any no harm, but don't spit it out too soon, 2 or 3 times a day is enough to use it, least it flea the skin off, and a little at a time is best.

We can see this recipe being carried out, the instructions are so clear. It was probably often needed. Salt prunella was made by melting salt petre and adding flowers of sulphur then burning to purify it.

CR80

The Opening Mixture

Take Senna leaves two Drachms, caraway Seeds one Drachm, Salt of Wormwood twenty Grains, Juice of Oinone a tablespoonfull; pour upon the Above rather more than a quarter of a pint of boiling Water. After one houre infusion strain it off, and to the strain'd Liquor Add two Table spoonfulls of Tincture of Senna, 6 Drachms of Rochelle Salts, or 4 Drachms of Glauber Salts. The dose, three or 4 Table spoonfulls.

This would certainly open the bowels. The caraway seeds are to ease griping pains from the action of the other ingredients. Rochelle and Glauber Salts are part of the fashionable chymical medicine. Earlier this century some alchemists became manufacturing chemists, one such, Johann Glauber, born 1603, discovered sodium sulphate in spring water. He later produced it as a by-product of making hydrochloric acid, named it

Glauber salt and claimed it would produce marvellous cures.

Rochelle salt was discovered by an apothecary in Rochelle in 1672. He advertised it as a laxative.

CR8O

The Emulsion

Spermaciti, one Drachm, Nitre, half a Drachm, fine Sugar, two or three Drachms. Beat all these together with the Yolk of an Egg, then gradually add near half a pint of Barley water. Give two spoonfulls every two or three hours.

Spermaceti is described by Quincy as more properly Oleum Ceti being an oil from the head of a particular sort of whale. He recommends it as safe and effectual in coughs, pleurisies and dysentery. Nitre, or salt-petre seems to have been imported largely from India for medicine, Quincy suspects it to have been obtained from the excrement of a large fowl. He writes it has greater repute as a universal medicine abroad.

CR8O

The Gargle for Mrs. Barnardiston.

Take one handfull of Black Currant leaves; put to it a pint of water boil'd down to a quarter of a pint; add to it one Table spoonfull of Honey & two Tea spoonfulls of Lemon Juice.

After the last recipe this tasty, homely, effective gargle is doubly welcome. It can be made with half a handful

141

of dried blackcurrant leaves in winter and is really soothing to the throat.

০৪৪০

The Bitter Draught or Bitter Potion

Take tops of ye Lesser Centry, & Camomil flowers, — of each a pugil, or so much as you can take up betwixt 3 fingers, Roots of Gentian half a scruple, Leaves of Senna, & seeds of carduns, of each a dram. Boyl them in sufficient qnty of fair water to 4 ounces or a quarter of a pint. If you would not have it purging, leave out ye Senna.

> Centaury (Centaurium erythraea) is a relatively gentle bitter suitable for children and used to stimulate the appetite, while Gentian (Gentiana lutea) is considerably stronger in action. The seeds of Carduus or milk thistle are included as a cleansing and protective treatment for the liver and spleen. It was seen as good for many digestive conditions. The chamomile would be additionally calming and soothing.

০৪৪০

Plasters for ye feet

Take a head of Garlick, & peal it, bruis it, & put it into a quarter of a pound of butter, & boyl them together well, & when cold spread it upon flannill & lay it on ye soles of ye feet. For a fever or vapours approv'd.

142

Applying slices of garlic to the feet was a good way of giving a slow-release dose. The effectiveness can be proven as the garlic permeates the body and the odour can be smelled on the breath. It used to be administered to children in this way for whooping cough.

CB80

A Dyett Drink for ye spring & fall
April & September

Take madder roots & monks Rheubarb of each six ounces; Scabiose, & Agrimony of each a large handfull; Licorice, Anniseed, Hermondactills, Sarsaparilla, Senna, of each two ounces. Scrape ye roots; bruise ye seeds & Hermondactills, & slice of Licorice. Putt these into two Gallons of new wort, of middle ale; but putt ye Senna by it self, & take it out in 4 days, & throw it away; but ye rest of ye ingredients will serve again, with ye Addition of New Senna. A Man or Woman may take two 3ds of a quart every morning; A Child of 7 or 8 years old half a pint.

This is clearly a recipe made and given regularly. Pechey records two opposite views on the action of madder roots, he finally includes both ideas and supposes it may act like the rhubarb in purging first and binding afterwards. Agrimony (Agrimonia eupatoria) was used in ill habits of the body for the liver and would be helpful in the stomach also. Liquorice (Glycyrrhiza glabra) was to gently loosen the belly and soothe "hot urine" as well as acting as an expectorant.

143

Senna would have been purgative, with aniseed to ease the griping. Culpeper writes of two Field Scabious and the corn scabious as having similar properties. It would appear to be contributing cleansing for the chest or inward ulcers here. The hermondactills sound mythical and were the cause of great discussion as to what exactly they were. Even Quincy's Dispensatory records the possibilities of colchicum, cyclamen, Iris tuberosa or a species of Dens Caninus. The confusion arose because they were imported from Turkey. All agreed their action was strongly purgative and helpful for gout and rheumatism.

C380

To make ye horse dunge water

Take horse dunge & putt to it so much Ale as will make it like hasty puding, and put it into your still. Then putt on ye topp one pound of treakell, and a quarter of a pound of genger an powder, and a quarter of a pound of sweet anniseeds, and so distill all these together. This water is good for women in labor and in childbed, for Agues and feavers and all distempers.

At least the ginger and aniseeds might cover for whatever flavour came from the horse dung! We cannot help but feel sorry for the patient drinking this, but perhaps they were unaware of the ingredients. If they did they must have been thankful it was distilled.

C380

Good in a fitt of ye Collick

To take a great quantity of Chicken broth, a gallon or more .

A fitting end to the section!

ఃಀ

Bibliography

Explanatory material in the physic section has been extracted from the following:

Buchan, W. 1776. *Domestic Medicine or a Treatise on the Prevention and Cure of Diseases,* (Appendix containing a Dispensatory). London.

Culpeper, N. 1815 edition. *Complete Herbal and English Physician* Enlarged, Richard Evans, London.

Edwards H.M., Vavasseur, P. 1829. *A Manual of Materia Medica and Pharmacy,* Philadelphia.

Fluckiger, F.A., Hanbury, D. 1879. *Pharmacographia. A History of The Principal Drugs of vegetable Origin met with in Great Britain and British India,* London.

Hill, John 1814. *The Family Herbal,* 1st edition 1754.

Johnson, T. (ed) 1975. *The Herbal,* Dover Publications, New York. (Gerard).

LaWall, C.H. 1927. *Four Thousand Years of Pharmacy,* Lippincott, London.

Lewer, H.W. (ed), 1908. *A Book of Simples,* Sampson Low, Marston & Co, London.

Miller, Joseph 1722. *Botanicum Officinale or a Compendious Herbal,* London.

Pechey, John 1694. *The English Herbal,* London.

Quincy, John 1736. *A Complete English Dispensatory,* London.

CB&O